Simplicity

Simplicity

◆

Finding Order, Freedom, and Fulfillment for Your Life

◆

Edward G. Dobson

ZondervanPublishingHouse

Grand Rapids, Michigan

A Division of HarperCollinsPublishers

Simplicity
Copyright ©1995 by Edward G. Dobson

Requests for information should be addressed to:

ZondervanPublishingHouse
Grand Rapids, Michigan 49530

Library of Congress Cataloging-in-Publication Data

Dobson, Ed.
    Simplicity : finding order, freedom, and fulfillment for your life / Edward G.
Dobson.
        p.   cm.
    Includes bibliographical references.
    ISBN 0-310-48701-3
    1. Simplicity—Religious aspects—Christianity. 2. Christian life.   I. Title.
BV4647.S48D63   1995
241'.4—dc 20   95–25512
                                                                          CIP

The names of some individuals have been changed in this book to protect their privacy.

Edited by Laura Weller

Interior design by Sue Koppenol

Printed in the United States of America

96 97 98 99 00 01 02 /❖ DH/ 10 9 8 7 6 5 4 3 2

Contents

◆

Preface

Of all the dissertations, magazine articles, and books I have written, this book has been the most difficult. The difficulty was twofold. First, I knew that writing this book would force me to take the next steps in my own journey toward a simpler life, so I kept delaying the actual writing. And in so doing, I was delaying my obligation to practice what I was about to write.

The second difficulty was the pace of daily life. I did not finish the book by the deadline I had agreed to. In fact, I missed deadline after deadline. Whenever a deadline was imminent, the pressure of pastoral ministry robbed me of study and writing time. On one occasion I blocked a whole week of vacation to finish the book. That same week I conducted three funerals of members of our church. I worked every day that week and wrote nothing!

But finally I finished. As writing this book has reminded me of my need to simplify my life, I hope that reading it will both challenge and encourage you on your journey toward simplicity. I hope that your life will be less cluttered and more focused as a result of reading this book.

◆

Part 1

PURSUING THE ELUSIVE DREAM

◆

◆

Chapter 1

I'M RUNNING AS FAST AS I CAN

◆

Our family lived for two years in a log cabin on four-and-a-half acres of woods. The cabin was seventeen-hundred square feet—three bedrooms and a large family room-kitchen area. We heated with a woodstove in the winter and cut and hauled our own wood. We took the garbage to the dump once a week in our 1949 Studebaker truck. We grew some of our own vegetables in the garden. We watched deer run through the yard and saw calves born in the large pasture next to our property. As I sit and write I can still smell the fire and feel the warmth of our cabin.

I remember the summer night when we sat on the front porch and played Monopoly together by the light of a kerosene lamp. I remember the many days we played football in the front, the kids dodging trees as they ran different patterns. I remember the brilliant yellow, brown, and red colors of fall and the afternoons when we raked leaves together. I remember shoveling out the driveway when it snowed and hauling wood in the Studebaker. I remember the dogwood trees blooming in spring—dozens of them. I remember the clear evenings when we could almost touch the stars. And TV—well, the reception was pretty poor, and with no cable the selections were limited.

There was something about the log cabin that contrasted with the rest of our lives. It was like a haven. I don't know if it was the setting, the smell of the logs, or the smallness of the house, but when we walked in we immediately relaxed. In the winter I would walk to the woodstove, turn the fan on high, and warm up my backside. In the winter the cabin was warm. In the summer it was cool. Whatever the season, it was always beautiful. Life seemed a lot simpler then.

That was then, but now is now. The house is bigger, and the children are growing up. We have guitar lessons, piano lessons, and gymnastics classes to attend. We go snow skiing and water skiing and play T-ball and soccer. We are involved in so many school and church activities that one family member walks in as another walks out. Rare are the times when enough of us can get together to play Monopoly.

Then there are my responsibilities at the church. My schedule is like a treadmill that somebody keeps turning up faster and faster. At first I preached one sermon on Sunday morning and one on Sunday night. Now I preach one sermon on Saturday night, three on Sunday morning, one on Sunday night, and one on Wednesday. I'm like a preaching machine. Wind me up and turn me loose. And all the meetings—give me a break!

That is not to say that life in the log cabin didn't have its share of complications. It did. The roof leaked, so when it rained we had pots and pans all over the living room. We had to spray for bugs once a month—an awful odor that lasted a couple of days. There was little privacy—you could hear anyone speak anywhere in the cabin. Every month I crawled under the house through red dirt to change the water filter and got soaked with water every time. But in spite of these things, it was a quiet center that brought a degree of tranquility to our lives. This book is about the journey toward that center—a place of tranquility and simplicity, a place we can reach by living out the principles God has set forth in his Word.

DAD, ARE YOU IN THERE?

My youngest child, Daniel, is eight years old. He is a bundle of energy and a truckload of questions and comments. Right now our favorite game is tickling each other. I call him the "tickle-master." We have "championship" tickle fights from the "Felt Forum" in Belmont, Michigan. When I walk in the door he runs to tickle me. When I lie down with him at night, we have "the last tickle of the day."

In between all the tickles he loves to talk. And when he talks he expects me to listen attentively, which I often forget. I'll be reading the paper or watching TV while he talks away about some subject. If he surmises that I'm half listening or not listening at all, he will walk over to me, wave his hand in front of my eyes, and say, "Dad, are you in there?" And then we have a tickle fight.

The truth is that I treat a lot of people that way—my wife, my children, my colleagues, my friends, and the many people I meet with daily. I don't listen. I'm so preoccupied with other matters that I don't give people full attention. Urban T. Holmes III writes about this in the book *Spirituality for Ministry*.

Many persons, ordained or not, live in a fairly constant state of noise, with their unresolved past and the uncertain present breaking in on them. They lack a still center and it is only for such a quiet point that we can listen attentively. When I was in my first parish, which was located in the middle of the city, a constant stream of indigents came through. One came into my office and wanted to tell me his story. I sat as if to listen but was deeply troubled inside over some issue now long forgotten. I remember I was fiddling with a pencil. The man stopped his story, looked at me and said, "Young

Father, the least you can do is listen." He was right. There was no still center in me.[1]

At times my life is the same way. As I sit and listen to a person pour out his or her heart, I may really be thinking of the next appointment or of the Sunday sermon. And what is true of that moment tends to be true of my life. It is a blur of activities. In the middle of one activity I'm thinking of the next, and when the day or the week or the year is done, I haven't really given my attention to much of anything. I'm existing—not living.

DIGGING GRAVES IS NOT COMPLICATED

There was a time when my life was not so complicated. Lorna and I got married a few days after we graduated from college. I felt my calling in life was to be an evangelist, so we started the Eddie Dobson Evangelistic Association. I chose the name Eddie instead of Ed or Edward because it sounded more like the name Billy—as in Graham. A few evangelistic meetings were planned for after we were married.

We sent several hundred letters to pastors and churches, but no one was interested. I felt like I was experiencing the words of the evil spirit who said, "Jesus I know, and I know about Paul, but who are you?" (Acts 19:15). My dreams of evangelism didn't last long. I had to get a job, and fortunately my brother-in-law offered me a job with his grave-digging company. So with my company-issued uniform, hard hat, and work boots, I began my career as a grave digger.

Actually, it was a pretty good job. The hours were steady (8:00–5:00). Necessary skills were minimal—digging, pushing a wheelbarrow, setting up funeral tents, and covering graves. Not much could go wrong, and the job didn't demand a lot of creative energy. Nobody really talked to me other than my fellow grave digger. In fact, when I attended social functions outside the business and people found out that I dug graves, they would usually leave me standing there alone.

Life was a lot simpler then: Get up. Go to work. Dig graves. Come home. Eat supper. Spend time with Lorna. Go to bed. Get up and do it over again. The phone never rang in the middle of the night. I had no meetings to attend, no children to chauffeur, no critical letters to answer. I had few expectations to meet and a lot of freedom to enjoy. So why not go back to just Lorna and me and digging graves? Sometimes I think, *That's not a bad idea!* But what would we do with the kids?

SOME PEOPLE SEEM TO HAVE A HANDLE ON SIMPLICITY

I have read about and met some people who seem to have a handle on the idea of simplicity. Dr. George Sheehan, writer, physician, and running guru, has some simple rules for each day: "No lunch, no novels, little T.V., a rare movie, few magazines, a quick pass through the newspaper."[2]

One modern group of Christians who seem to have embraced material simplicity is missionaries. I have traveled to various countries to partnership with missionaries in outreach. I once spent several days with Carole Jamieson and her family in a remote Indian village in the mountains of Mexico. She and her late husband and family had spent twenty-five years working and living with these Indians. They learned their language, committed it to writing, taught the people to read, and translated the New Testament into their dialect. I was there for the fiesta that celebrated the completion of the project and its distribution.

The Jamiesons lived in a home with a dirt floor. Every day the water was carried up from the river (thirty minutes down and two hours back). Because of the toil involved in getting water, the toilet was flushed only once a day. They had a primitive lifestyle far removed from the complexities of the United States.

I also spent a week with Pablo and Karen Riguero in their tiny fourth-floor apartment in Barcelona, Spain. Pablo pastors a growing church at the foot of Olympic Mountain. While they have a television, a refrigerator, and three bedrooms, their lifestyle is a long way from that of the average family in our church. I could continue this list—from crowded apartments in Taiwan to huts in remote villages missionaries live a radically altered lifestyle from our own.

SIMPLICITY IS NOT ALL THAT SIMPLE

When I read the writings of those who have found simplicity or visit with people in other cultures who live simply, I am both encouraged and discouraged—encouraged because people don't have to live the way we do, discouraged because I find it difficult to transfer these lifestyles to Grand Rapids, Michigan. I do not identify with missionaries because I am not a missionary, I live in a nice home, I drive a good car, and I am paid a good salary. So what do I do? Sell it all, kiss my job good-by, and go live in a developing country?

Simplicity is not that simple. It is neither simple to define nor to put into practice. Thus running away to some quiet, remote location is not the answer to simplifying our hectic lives.

So what is simplicity? Consider the elements that Webster identifies in his definition.

1. *The state of being simple or uncompounded.* Compound interest is interest that is continually added to the principal—layer after layer after layer. Simplicity is freedom from compounded interest, or the refusal to add unnecessary layers to our lives.

2. *Lack of subtlety or penetration.* A subtle person is one who has hidden motives or interests. Penetration means going beneath the surface. Simplicity is a state of complete openness where

there are no hidden agendas, motives, or interests beneath the surface. What you see is what you get.

3. *Freedom from pretense or guile.* Pretense is pretending to be something or someone you are not. It is playing roles to impress or manipulate others. Simplicity is being yourself.

4. *Directness of expression.* People often say what others want to hear or refuse to say what others need to hear for fear of the consequences. Simplicity is speaking the truth.

5. *Restraint in ornamentation.* We have lots of ornaments: watches, rings, jewelry, clothes, cars, houses, and so on. We tend to buy these things to impress others. Simplicity is restraint, the refusal to keep up with the Joneses.

Webster includes words like *innocence, naivete, candor, clarity, austerity,* and *streamline* to describe simplicity. Albert E. Day, in his book *Discipline and Discovery*, says that simplicity means "absence of artificial ornamentation, pretentious styles, or luxury. . . . Where there is simplicity, words can be taken at their face value. There is no hidden or double meanings. . . . Where there is simplicity there is no artificiality. One does not try to appear younger, or wiser, or richer than one is—or more saintly."[3] Richard Foster, in *Celebration of Discipline,* puts it in "simple" language. "Simplicity is freedom. Duplicity is bondage. Simplicity brings joy and balance. Duplicity brings anxiety and fear."[4] Foster distinguishes between the inward reality of simplicity and the outward experience of simplicity. We tend to focus on the outward: What clothes should I buy? What car should I drive? What house should I live in? Outward simplicity without inward simplicity only leads to superficial legalism (sets of rules about lifestyle). However, genuine inward simplicity will lead to properly motivated outward simplicity, which leads to liberty—not legalism.

Simplicity is fundamentally a process of getting rid of the duplicity in our lives—both inward and outward. It is the process of downward mobility, in which we constantly refuse to be caught up in the game of accumulation and status. It is the process of paying attention to our inward tranquility as opposed to only responding to the external pressures that drive us to exhaustion. It involves our relationship to God as well as to others. It includes our attitudes, actions, conversations, and emotions. It includes our cars, homes, clothes, and material possessions. It includes all of this and more.

In the following chapters I have attempted to explore most of these areas. Perhaps you have a handle on some of them already. I find that my challenge is to keep them all in balance. About the time I make some progress in outward simplicity, my inward simplicity starts to slide, and vice versa. But that's okay. I refuse to carry the guilt of not having my act together. After all, simplicity is a process.

SIMPLICITY IS GETTING RID OF THE FIG LEAVES

As human beings we were created to enjoy life with the simplicity of children—children of God. Scripture says, "God made man simple; man's complex problems are of his own doing" (Eccl. 7:30 JB). When God created Adam and Eve he placed them in a perfect environment to enjoy God and each other. The instructions were simple:

1. Be fruitful and increase in number.
2. Rule over creation.
3. Work and take care of the garden.
4. Don't eat of the Tree of the Knowledge of Good and Evil.

This was utopia—a simple, uncomplicated life. Adam and Eve had a great relationship.

Adam and Eve were naked and felt no shame (Gen. 2:25). They had a relationship without duplicity—an open, honest, vulnerable relationship with nothing to hide. The same was true of their relationship with God.

Then it happened: They complicated their lives by disobeying God. After they had eaten of the tree, two things happened. First, their eyes were opened and they realized they were naked, so they sewed fig leaves together to cover themselves. They began adding layers of stuff to hide from each other. Second, they hid from God among the trees of the garden. Their simplicity and openness had been shattered. They were now hiding from each other and God. And so goes the history of humanity. We have been adding layers of fig leaves to hide from each other and finding forests of trees in which to hide from God. Simplicity is getting rid of the fig leaves, the duplicity that compounds our lives. It is also coming out of the forest and living before God with authenticity.

But coming out of the forest and living with authenticity and transparency before God and others can be a frightening prospect. It is much easier to hide. Often the fears of being honest and letting people see the real "us" prevents us from getting rid of the fig leaves. In fact, it is much easier to keep on adding layers than it is to peel off layers. Adding is our natural instinct. Subtracting requires supernatural assistance. Adding enslaves us to the clutter of life. Subtracting sets us free.

◆

Chapter 2

SIMPLICITY: TO DREAM THE IMPOSSIBLE DREAM

◆

The sick man, wasted by fever, consumed with thirst, dreams in his sleep of a fresh stream wherein he bathes, or of a clear fountain from which he drinks in great droughts. So, amid the confused restlessness of modern life, our wearied minds dream of simplicity.

CHARLES WAGNER
PARIS, 1895[1]

What strikes me most about the above statement is that it was written more than a hundred years ago! It was written by a French Lutheran pastor before the invention of the light bulb, the telephone, the car, the refrigerator, the airplane, the television, the computer, the microwave, the fax machine, and scores of other now-common conventions. We would call Wagner's world pre-

modern, yet he described his time as one of "confused restlessness" filled with "wearied minds." A hundred years later we are
more confused, more restless, and more wearied—and we still
dream of simplicity.

BEING BORN IS COMPLICATED

I was born on December 30, 1949, outside Magherafelt in
Belfast, Northern Ireland. I was not born in a hospital, and my
parents had never heard of Lamaze. I was born at home, a one-
room, whitewashed thatched cottage. The walls were made of
stone, and the roof was made of hay. The house was heated by an
open hearth that was also used for cooking. The toilet—well, it
was down the path a wee bit. No doctors, nurses, or photographers
attended my birth, only a midwife. But I made it.

Times have changed. My three children were born in Lynchburg, Virginia, at the Virginia Baptist Hospital, and they all were
delivered by the same doctor. As a dutiful, modern husband, I
attended birthing classes with my wife. We learned about the pre-
natal development of babies, the birthing process, and other related
topics. My wife, Lorna, learned how to handle her contractions by
controlled breathing and how to focus to ease the pain. I was her
coach. It was my job to time her contractions, offer encouragement,
and, when necessary, get out of the way. Our birthing experience was
far from my parents' experience in the thatched cottage in Ireland.
Surrounded by doctors, nurses, and state-of-the-art technology, our
children—Kent, Heather, and Daniel—entered the modern world.
As time passes, more and more options are open to couples, and the
birth process becomes even more complicated.

EVEN DYING CAN BE COMPLICATED

The Irish are wonderful storytellers. My mind is filled with
stories I heard over a cup of tea poured from a pot brewed on an

open hearth. One story is about three old bachelor brothers. One was on his death bed, and the other two were discussing the funeral arrangements.

"It's so expensive to get a funeral director these days," one said.

"Aye," said the other. "Maybe we can do it ourselves. We'll just carry him on the cart up to the cemetery."

"What about a coffin? They're awfully dear, you know."

"Aye, maybe we could use an orange crate out of the barn."

"Good idea. But what about the grave?"

"Well, we could find a corner in the pasture and dig the hole ourselves."

As they continued discussing how they could save more money, a weak voice spoke up from the bed, "If you'll give me my pants, I'll walk!"

Even dying is no longer simple. As a pastor I have stood beside the beds of people who were kept alive by modern medicine but were doomed to a life of pain, suffering, and great limitation. I have also stood by the beds of babies, young people, and adults who were on life-support systems. I have prayed and talked with their families about whether or not to unplug the machines. These decisions are heart wrenching and complex. Years ago when it was time to go, you went. Today modern technology often complicates the dying process.

If being born is complicated and dying is complicated, you can be sure that everything else in between is complicated as well. As Wagner said it, "From the cradle to the grave, in his needs as in his pleasures, in his conception of the world and of himself, the man of modern times struggles through a maze of endless complications. Nothing is simple any longer: neither thought nor action, not pleasure, not even dying."[2]

CAN LIFE BE SIMPLIFIED?

Life at best is complex, and Christians are not immune to this complexity. June McEwen, in her book *The Gift of Simplicity,* lists a series of questions that help identify this complexity in reference to family life. The following is a partial list of these questions:

- Why do Christian familes often operate in an atmosphere of impatience and irritability?
- Why do Christian families feel pressured to add to their material possessions?
- Why do they feel trapped by a spirit of need for more and more things?
- Why are Christian families oppressed by bad money management?
- Why are there too many bills to pay, too little savings, too little to give away to others?
- Why do Christian families overschedule their time?
- Why do they leave little time for prayer?
- Why is there no time for solitude, meditation, and contemplation in the lives of most people today?
- Why do Christian families succumb to burnout, stress reactions, and broken relationships?
- Why is there inadequate communication, too much anger and guilt?
- Why are Christians burdened down by resentment, anxiety, worry, and depression?
- Why are Christians nearly powerless on issues such as the quality of movies, books, and drama?
- Why are they deluged by effects of advertisement in so many of the daily choices they make?
- Why are Christians affected more and more by popular cultural value systems?

- Why are Christians increasingly traumatized by the reports on the nightly news on television?
- Why are Christian families so often torn between opinions and courses of action?[3]

Why? Why? Why? Why? In the face of these unanswered questions and the blur of activities and obligations of daily living, can we begin to simplify our lives? I wish I could answer with a resounding and emphatic, "YES WE CAN!" The most I can do is whisper quietly, "Maybe" or "Maybe not!"

In dealing with the challenges of simplifying life, some people have become models of success. They took radical action to alter either their vocation or location in order to simplify their lives. Perhaps the most famous was Ralph Waldo Emerson. Many others have followed in his footsteps. Frank Levering, a Hollywood screen writer, and his wife, Wanda Urbanska, a young journalist, shunned the fast life of Los Angeles and moved to the mountains of Virginia to run the family orchard. They tell their story in a book entitled *Simple Living*. In the process of simplification they discovered "freedom from the tyranny of never having enough time and freedom to do things [their] own way."[4] They talk about taking Sunday off as a day of rest, refusing to eat out at restaurants in order to save money, not purchasing anything unless the cash was in hand, and continuing to drive an old car instead of buying a new one.

> Here in Virginia we have discovered that—though no one is ever free of contradictions—one *can* change the general direction of one's life, can make it simpler and more satisfying in a range of important respects. With us, because we found no quick fixes, because our lives hold the potential for as much complexity at the orchard as they had in Los Angeles, change has not happened overnight or without a small mountain of struggle. But we have changed, and we

continue to change as we hone our desires and pursue goals that bring our lives and ideals into closer alignment.[5]

The following excerpts from Niall Williams and Christine Breen's diaries in their book *When Summer's in the Meadow* tell the idyllic story of returning to Ireland to live in a cottage and farm the land.

It was raining softly. I was standing at the gate to the back meadow in the early morning, gazing up across the hill fields of Tumper. Nothing was moving. No sound came or went on the Kiltumper road. A pale gray sky seemed to sit down, drizzling, over the day. . . . It had already been a year and a half since we moved here from New York, and now the tremendous silence of these wet November days was shaped by each morning's writing in the parlor and the watching, feeding, and herding of Susie, Phoebe, Bridget and Gerty, our cows. . . .

When I think of the things I *have* learned since coming to Ireland . . . I could make a list of them that would fill a book! From using spent chicken manure in the garden to boiling the kettle on the open fire, from baking brown bread scones to dehorning calves, from "footing" turf to "earthing up" potatoes, from designing sets for the drama group to fattening turkeys. And painting, in itself, has been quite a learning process too. Like everything else, it takes time. Discoveries come slowly. . . .

Niall and I worked in different parts of the garden; he dug potato ridges, and I weeded the flower borders. The sun was shining in a clear blue sky. Our arms were bare to the warm air. What more could we ask for? I had such a feeling of wholeness and happiness. I hope in the years to come I can look back on this day and remember how good it is.[6]

This delightful book about the simple life in Ireland touched the core of my being. I felt the rain. I smelled the scones baking. I saw the green meadows. And I longed for a life of simplicity.

But as inspirational as the stories of those who have walked away from the rat race are, most of us cannot walk away and start over. The lure of an Irish cottage sounds good, but the reality is often different. My uncle is a farmer in Ireland. Recently he fell off the barn into a large pile of manure and was seriously hurt. He works from early morning until late at night every day. He is in a constant struggle with the weather, the crops, the animals, and his workers. Most people can return to Walden Pond only in their minds.

Two fundamental problems exist with returning to Walden Pond. First, this kind of radical change deals primarily with material simplicity. It does not deal with the other pressing areas of emotional simplicity, spiritual simplicity, and relational simplicity. Second, few people have the courage, the resources, or the opportunity to make such changes. So what can we do? First we must understand that there are two major obstacles that we must confront.

Obstacle 1: Excess Baggage

Shortly after Lorna and I were married we moved from Greenville, South Carolina, to Lynchburg, Virginia. We rented the smallest U-Haul trailer available and brought *all* our belongings—clothes, wedding presents, and one piece of furniture—with us. When we moved from Lynchburg to Grand Rapids, Michigan, we needed a full-sized semi-trailer to haul our belongings. In less than fifteen years, along with adding three children, a dog, and a cat to our family, we had accumulated far more stuff than we needed. We brought it all to Michigan and have amassed even more since then.

One of the obstacles to simplicity is the junk we have gathered over the years. I'm not referring only to material things. Over the years we collect rooms full of emotional baggage—pain, disappointment, abuse, broken relationships. We also pile up spiritual baggage—disobedience, guilt, legalism. The list goes on and on. If we are to begin our journey toward simplicity, we must be willing to open up the cluttered rooms of our lives and throw out the junk.

Obstacle 2: Disparity Between Our Lives and Our Ideals

A second obstacle to simplicity is the growing gulf between our ideals and our daily living. Frank Levering and Wanda Urbanska have written of their experience in simplification, "But we have changed, and we continue to change as we hone our desires and ideals into closer alignment."[7]

Take a moment to think about your ideals. What is important to you? What goals have top priority? A time of reflection will reveal a partial list of ideals. My list is short:

- Have a healthy relationship with God.
- Have an intimate relationship with my wife.
- Be a good father.
- Be a good pastor.

However, when I examine the reality of my daily activities, I discover a gap between my ideals and the way I actually live. And to further complicate the problem, I am too busy existing to spend much time realigning my ideals with my life!

A WORD OF CAUTION

The journey toward a simpler life is both long and difficult. The pressures of life around us constantly push us in the wrong direction. The expectations we put on ourselves as well as those others place on us mitigate against a simpler life. To change ourselves and our lives for the better will demand unusual courage, continual vigilance, honest self-examination, and intense persistence.

Chapter 3

READY, FIRE, AIM!

Most of us lead lives that two hours' reflection would lead us to disown.

ROBERT LOUIS STEVENSON

TAKING AIM TAKES TIME

I conduct about twenty-five funerals a year. In the past eight years I have met with more than two hundred families and have helped them plan a memorial service as well as deal with their grief. The most unusual service I have ever conducted was for the Michigan Funeral Directors' Association. At the annual meeting of all the funeral directors in the state, a memorial service is held to honor their own people who have died in the last year.

It was a very moving service. Before I spoke someone showed a slide presentation with photographs and information on everyone in the association who had died in the last year. By the time I got up to speak many people were crying. I talked to them about the difference between facing death on a professional level and facing death on a personal level. I told them that when one comes to the end of his or her earthly journey, only two things really matter: first, one's relationship with God, and second, one's relationship to others—especially one's family.

I talked about the importance of facing life by first of all facing death. What most of us think is important today is not all that important when placed against the reality of our own mortality. At the end of the journey it is not all that important what we did for a living, what kind of home we lived in, what clothes we wore, what car we drove, or what awards we won. What matters is our relationship to God and the investment we have made in our family and in other people. I concluded the talk by asking them to spend time each day reading the Bible and to go home and hug their spouse and children.

Even though we know we are going to die, and even though we know what is truly important, we too often neglect it for the pressure of the immediate. We live by the motto: "Ready, fire, aim!" One thing about taking aim is that it requires thought and reflection. It requires identifying what is truly important and rearranging our lives. It requires constant diligence to resist secondary priorities. It requires learning to say yes and learning to say no. It requires continuous review and adjustment. And all of this requires time.

To insure that his disciples took time to refocus, Jesus called them away from the crowds to whom they had been busy ministering. He said, "Come with me by yourselves to a quiet place and get some rest" (Mark 6:31). And he calls us today to do the same.

WHAT DOES IT MEAN TO TAKE AIM?

Stephen R. Covey, in his best-selling book *The Seven Habits of Highly Effective People,* discusses the concept of "taking aim." He calls this idea "Beginning with the end in mind" (Habit 2). He writes:

> To begin with the end in mind means to start with a
> clear understanding of your destination. It means to know

where you're going so that you better understand where you are now and so that the steps you take are always in the right direction.

It's incredibly easy to get caught up in an activity trap, in the busy-ness of life, to work harder and harder at climbing the ladder of success, only to discover it's leaning against the wrong wall. It is possible to be busy—very busy—without being very effective.[1]

So how do we take aim? How do we identify "the end" so that we can shape our daily lives with deliberate purpose? Four steps will facilitate this process. Each step takes time and effort.

1. Facing our own mortality
2. Identifying and reflecting on who we are as human beings
3. Identifying the roles we play
4. Developing a simple mission statement

Step 1: Facing Our Own Mortality

Human beings are good at making plans and setting goals. We keep daily appointment books and set weekly, monthly, and yearly goals. We plan our business, our family life, and our vacations, but we seldom plan for eternity. Even though we believe in eternity and know that it is our final destination, that knowledge seldom influences our daily choices. Still the Bible admonishes us to live each day with eternal values in view (James 4:13–17). How do we do this? We begin by coming to terms with a biblical view of life and a biblical view of eternity.

A Biblical View of Life

The Bible repeatedly reminds us that life is brief. It is here today and gone tomorrow. Life is like the time of twilight between sunshine and darkness or like the grass that is green one day and burnt by the sun the next (Ps. 102:11). It is like a flower that blooms. The wind blows over it, and it is gone and no one remembers it (Ps. 103:15–16). Life is like a breath. We breathe in and breathe out, and life is over (Job 7:7). It is like a cloud that appears for a moment and then is gone (Job 7:9–10). There are no guarantees for tomorrow. Scripture warns, "Do not boast about tomorrow, for you do not know what a day may bring forth" (Prov. 27:1; cf. James 4:14).

A Biblical View of Eternity

"Man is destined to die once, and after that to face judgment" (Heb. 9:27). This life is not all there is. The Bible clearly teaches that there are two eternal destinations: heaven and hell. Both are real and forever. Unfortunately, we live as if heaven is a fairy tale and hell does not exist. When facing God and eternity only two questions will really matter: (1) What did I do with Jesus, and (2) What did I do with my life (my service for Jesus)?

Step 2: Identifying and Reflecting on Who We Are As Human Beings

We can reflect on our humanity in two ways. First, we can consider our basic human nature. We are physical, emotional, and spiritual beings. Second, we can consider our humanity in its various relationships. We have relationships with ourselves, others, and God.

Our Human Nature

Theologians love to debate whether human beings are dichotomist beings or trichotomist beings—that is, do human beings have two parts or three parts? Are we material and immaterial (dichotomist), or are we body, soul, and spirit (trichotomist)? The answer is both. We are both material and immaterial, and we are body, soul, and spirit. First, we are physical beings. We have a body. How we treat our body determines the quality of our life. We can do positive things to enhance our health, such as eating a balanced diet and getting proper rest and exercise. Or we can do negative things that will rob us of good health, such as overeating, abusing drugs and alcohol, or smoking.

Second, we are emotional beings. We have a soul, which includes our mind, emotions, and will. We are not just physical bodies preprogrammed to act alike. Each of us has a personality. We have a mind to make decisions. We have feelings over which we have control. We have the ability to make choices. And we all are different. No two human beings are alike.

Third, we are spiritual beings. We have a spirit. We were created with the capacity to have a relationship with our Creator, and we are incomplete until we find that relationship.

We are body, soul, and spirit. We are physical, emotional, and spiritual beings. The following diagram illustrates:

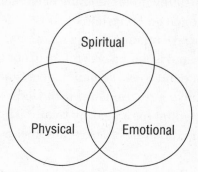

Note three things about this diagram. First, the three areas are interconnected. They are not separate and freestanding. Second, these areas have direct impact on each other. For example, if I am physically ill (a body problem), my illness can impact my emotions (depression) and my spirit (I may not feel like praying). Third, in dealing with problems, I must explore the root issue, not just the symptoms. For example, if I do not feel like praying, it may not be a spiritual problem at all. I may be physically ill. Only when I deal with the root issue (sickness) will the spiritual issue (I don't feel like praying) be resolved.

Our Human Relationships

The second way to understand our humanity is to understand it within the context of human relationships. These relationships can be divided three ways—a relationship with ourselves, a relationship with others, and a relationship with God. I have listed these relationships in the chronological order in which they develop. First, we have a relationship with ourselves, feelings about who we are. Numerous words can be used to describe this relationship: *self-worth*—the value we place on ourselves; *self-acceptance*—accepting who we are; *self-image*—how we feel about ourselves; *self-love*—how we care for ourselves. Research indicates that a healthy understanding of our self-relationship is vital to our emotional and physical health.

Second, we have relationships with others. We do not live in monastic silence and isolation. We relate to our families, friends, neighbors, fellow employees, acquaintances, and even strangers.

Third, we have a relationship with God—that is, we have the need and potential for a healthy relationship with God. The following diagram illustrates these relationships:

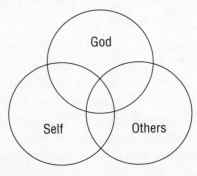

Note that these relationships are interconnected rather than separate and freestanding. They have direct impact on each other. For example, if I have a poor self-image that comes from my father's verbal abuse, I may have difficulty relating to God as my kind "heavenly Father." And my poor self-image may cause me to try to earn others' approval by performance since I believe they would never accept me as I am.

Now that we can see that we are physical, emotional, and spiritual beings in relationship with ourselves, others, and God, let us "take aim" at this definition. What is of vital importance in these areas of my life? What are my long-term goals for these areas? When I come to the end of my life, what do I want people to say about me? Let me encourage you at this point to do the following assignment: Consider each of the following categories and ask two questions. First, what is the current status of this area of my life? (In other words, "How am I doing?") Second, what would be ideal? (In other words, "What should I be doing if I had the time and energy?") Answer each question with a one-sentence response.

- Physical
  What is the current status? _____
  What would be ideal? _____

- Emotional
  What is the current status? _____
  What would be ideal? _____

- Spiritual
  What is the current status? _____
  What would be ideal? _____

- Self
  What is the current status? _____
  What would be ideal? _____

- Others
  What is the current status? _____
  What would be ideal? _____

- God
  What is the current status? _____
  What would be ideal? _____

Step 3: Identifying the Roles We Play

In addition to understanding who we are as human beings, we must also consider the various roles we play. Some of these roles we choose; others are chosen for us. But all are important, and each makes demands of our time and energy. On a separate piece of paper or in the space provided below, list the various roles you play. Again, ask two basic questions of each role. First, what is the current status of this role? Second, what would be ideal? Answer each question with a one-sentence response. The following is a partial list.

- Spouse
  What is the current status? _____
  What would be ideal? _____

- Parent
  What is the current status? _____
  What would be ideal? _____

- Child
  What is the current status? _____
  What would be ideal? _____

- Sibling
  What is the current status? _____
  What would be ideal? _____

- Employee/Employer
  What is the current status? _____
  What would be ideal? _____

- Friend
  What is the current status? _____
  What would be ideal? _____

These roles all demand time and energy, and they all impact each other. Together they form the essence of our daily living.

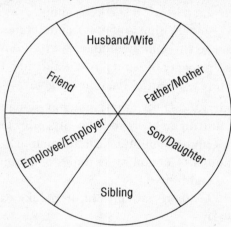

Step 4: Developing a Mission Statement

Having found out who we are as human beings and the roles we play, it is now time to synthesize this material into a personal mission statement that "focuses on what you want to be (character) and to do (contributions and achievements) and on the values or principles upon which being and doing is based."[2]

There are a variety of ways to develop a personal mission statement. The first time I developed one for my own life was shortly after Christmas 1990. I was on my way to Mexico City to meet some missionaries. They were to take me to a remote Indian tribe in the nation of Mexico where I would help distribute the first New Testaments in their Indian dialect. Several weeks before the trip I had attended a time management seminar. Participants were encouraged to make time to write out a one-sentence personal mission statement. I decided that one of my goals for the Mexico trip was to come back with that statement.

I began by working through a process similar to the first three steps suggested above. Then I spent a lot of time reflecting and going over this information. Eventually (after many attempts), I produced this one-sentence personal mission statement: "I want to be a godly husband, father, and pastor." It seems so simple, yet it does reflect an attempt to take aim at what is of utmost importance in my life.

In addition to this one sentence, I wrote down some key areas/relationships of my life and put specific, ideal goals next to each of them. Here is a partial list of ideal goals.

- Spiritual walk: Daily quiet time, focus on prayer
- Physical: Run an average of twenty miles per week
- Personal improvement: Learn Spanish
- Recreational: Get golf score under one hundred (my first goal was eighty-five)
- Father: Play more with my children, take each child on a mission trip

I found this process to be most helpful. Each month I look back and rate myself in regard to my goals and objectives. A personal mission statement does not have to be a one-sentence statement; it can be a series of statements. Following are some examples of others' mission statements.

Thomas G. Pettepiece, in *Visions of a World Hungry*, identifies nine principles that he utilizes to guide his life. These principles represent serious thinking about what is truly important in life and set forth priorities so that one can keep on track each day.

1. I declare myself to be a world citizen.
2. I commit myself to lead an ecologically sound life.

3. I commit myself to lead a life of creative simplicity and to share my personal wealth with the world's poor.

4. I commit myself to join with others in reshaping institutions in order to bring about a more just global society in which each person has full access to the needed resources of their [sic] physical, emotional, intellectual, and spiritual growth.

5. I commit myself to occupational accountability, and in so doing I seek to avoid the creation of products which cause harm to others.

6. I affirm the gift of my body, and commit myself to its proper nourishment and physical well-being.

7. I commit myself to examine continually my relations with others, and to attempt to relate honestly, orally, and lovingly to those around me.

8. I commit myself to personal renewal through prayer, meditation, and study.

9. I commit myself to responsible participation in a community of faith.[3]

Jonathan Edwards, eighteenth-century American theologian, lived by a series of seventy resolutions, which he reviewed weekly. Here are the first ten:

1. Resolved, That I will do whatsoever I think to be most to the glory of God, and my own good, profit, and pleasure, in the whole of my duration; without any consideration of the time, whether now, or never so many myriads of ages hence. Resolved to do whatever I think to be my duty, and most for the good and advantage of mankind in general. Resolved, so to do, whatever difficulties I meet with, how many soever, and how great soever.

2. Resolved, To be continually endeavouring to find out some new contrivance and invention to promote the forementioned things.

3. Resolved, If ever I shall fall and grow dull, so as to neglect to keep any part of these Resolutions, to repent of all I can remember, when I come to myself again.

4. Resolved, Never to do any manner of thing, whether in soul or body, less or more, but what tends to the glory of God, nor be, nor suffer it, if I can possibly avoid it.

5. Resolved, Never to lose one moment of time, but to improve it in the most profitable way I possibly can.

6. Resolved, To live with all my might, while I do live.

7. Resolved, Never to do any thing, which I should be afraid to do if it were the last hour of my life.

8. Resolved, To act, in all respects, both speaking and doing, as if nobody had been so vile as I, and as if I had committed the same sins, or had the same infirmities or failings, as others; and that I will let the knowledge of their failings promote nothing but shame in myself, and prove only an occasion of my confessing my own sins and misery to God.

9. Resolved, To think much, on all occasions, of my dying, and of the common circumstances which attend death.

10. Resolved, When I feel pain, to think of the pains of martyrdom, and of hell.[4]

Simplicity begins with a deliberate attempt to bring focus and direction to one's life and relationships. It will not happen as part of a natural evolutionary process but will require careful and specific intervention. And it will require continual oversight and ongoing mid-course corrections to keep us on track.

A STRUCTURE FOR SIMPLICITY

The rest of this book is devoted to exploring, evaluating, and simplifying three general areas of our lives. First, it will deal with *inner* simplicity, which confronts the baggage we carry around inside of us. Second, it will deal with *outward* simplicity, which confronts the baggage we accumulate in our relationships with others. Third, it will deal with *upward* simplicity, which confronts the baggage we accumulate in our relationship with God. My goal is to encourage you to journey toward authenticity and simplicity in your personal life and in how you relate to others and to God.

◆

Part 2

FINDING INNER SIMPLICITY

◆

◆

Chapter 4

THE SIMPLICITY OF FORGIVENESS

◆

Not all Christians were silent during the dark days of the Nazi regime during World War II. Some Protestants and Catholics resisted and met the same fate as millions of Jews—execution. One such resister was Father Alfred Delp, who joined the secret discussions of the Kreisau Circle, an anti-Nazi group who saw the imminent demise of Nazism and began plans for implementing a new social order based on Christian principles after the war. Father Delp was arrested as one of the leaders, tried for treason, found "guilty" and executed in the Plotzensee prison on February 2, 1945. During his prison ordeal he kept a diary, which was published in German in 1956 and then in English in 1963.[1]

Shortly before his execution, Father Delp wrote some powerful words about forgiveness.

> Nor must I forget those to whom I owe so much. May those I have hurt forgive me—I am sorry for having injured them. May those to whom I have been untrue forgive me—

I am sorry for having failed them. May those to whom I have been proud and overbearing forgive me—I repent my arrogance. And may those to whom I have been unloving forgive me—I repent my hardness. Oh yes—long hours spent in this cell with fettered wrists and my body and spirit tormented must have broken down a great deal that was hard in me. Much that was unworthy and worthless has been committed to the flames.[2]

Delp was falsely accused, unfairly arrested, and unjustly condemned. His death was only days away. Yet in the face of death he was concerned about the people he had hurt and he wanted their forgiveness.

Journalist Terry Anderson was the longest-held American hostage in Lebanon. He endured six and a half years of imprisonment chained to a wall. After his release he was taken to Wiesbaden, Germany, where he held a press conference. Asked if he had ever given up hope, he replied, "There were some bad times. There were times I was in despair, but I don't think I was ever going to give up." He had found encouragement through reading the Bible.

Speaking of his captors, Anderson said: "I don't hate anybody. I'm a Christian and a Catholic, and I believe that it is required of me to forgive no matter how hard that is, and I am determined to do that." Forgiveness is not easy when you have been beaten, abused, and held against your will. Forgiveness is not easy when you have been deprived of freedom and family for six and a half years. But Terry Anderson was determined to forgive.

There was another man who was falsely arrested. He was condemned in a "kangaroo court" and sentenced to die in a most cruel and primitive way—crucifixion. Yet when the Roman soldiers drove nails into his hands and feet, his response was one of forgiveness. "Father, forgive them," he said, "for they do not know what they are doing" (Luke 23:34). His name was Jesus Christ.

"STICKS AND STONES MAY BREAK MY BONES, BUT NAMES WILL NEVER HURT ME"

Remember reciting this little poem as a kid when other kids called you names? You acted as if what they said didn't hurt you. Wrong! Nothing could have been further from the truth. Sticks and stones do hurt. Broken bones are painful. But bones heal. Name-calling hurts far more than broken bones. It cuts deep into our esteem and feelings and leaves wounds that remain open for years—sometimes for life.

One harsh reality of the world in which we live is that we will get hurt. The question is not *if* we'll get hurt; it's *when* we'll get hurt. After all, we live in an imperfect world of imperfect people who do imperfect things to each other. I wish I could be a perfect parent, but I'm not. I wish I could be a perfect husband, but I'm not. I wish I could live life without hurting people, but I can't. There are no perfect people, no perfect relationships, and no perfect institutions—including the church. Consequently, the overriding issue is not the reality of hurt, but rather how we will respond to it.

WHAT TO DO WHEN YOU GET "DONE"

We cannot control what others may do to us, nor can we build a strategic defense initiative that will protect us from the pain of what others do or say. What we can do, however, is control our response. We have choices about what to do.

Option 1: Repress the Hurt

When some people get hurt they simply bury their pain deep inside. They act as if nothing has happened. They grit their teeth and go on. The problem with burying hurt, however, is that we never bury our feelings dead—we only bury them alive. They don't go away, and instead they continue to eat away at our emotional health.

Anger turned inward can lead to bitterness, and bitterness can lead to depression.

I attended a very strict college. We had room inspection every day. The beds had to be made and the room cleaned. Early on I learned an important strategy. I got an extra-wide bedspread. When the bed was made the spread would go all the way to the floor. In the morning I would throw all the dirty clothes under the bed so that when the room was inspected nobody could see them. The dirty clothes were well hidden by the bedspread. The only problem was that if I left them there too long, they began to stink. In fact, my whole room smelled like a locker room.

The same is true with burying feelings. You can sweep your hurt feelings under the bed, but like dirty socks, they will stink and mess up your entire life. They won't go away; they'll only get worse.

Option 2: Express the Hurt

"I don't get mad; I get even." How often have you heard that statement? It certainly is one option you have when you get hurt. If someone hurts you, give that person a piece of your mind. Blow up. Yell. Get it out of your system.

Expressing your feelings has a great advantage: It allows you to release the pressure of the hurt and makes you feel good. However, it also has a major disadvantage: It usually hurts the person on whom you ventilate.

Picture this scenario. Dad goes to work, and the boss blows up at him. Even though Dad would like to retaliate, it isn't safe to yell at the boss. So he swallows (represses) his feelings and goes on. But anger builds each time he thinks about the incident. When he gets home, dinner is not quite ready.

"Honey, how come dinner isn't ready?" he asks his wife. "What have you been doing all day?"

She hasn't had a spare minute all day, so her husband's questioning sends her over the edge. She is mad, but she swallows her anger and curses him under her breath.

In walks one of the kids with mud on her sneakers. Mom has had enough!

"Mary, how many times have I told you to take your dirty shoes off at the door?" she storms. "I'm sick and tired of you not listening to me. Go to your room. You're grounded for a week!"

Poor Mary. She is mad at her mother but doesn't dare talk back. That would mean grounding for a year, not a week. On the way to her room she kicks Fido, the dog. He was just lying there doing nothing, but now he's mad. He takes off after the cat, who runs through the den and jumps into Dad's lap while he is reading the paper. Dad gets mad. "What's wrong with these animals?" he yells in disgust.

What's wrong? Everybody is repressing and then expressing their feelings. And the chain reaction goes on and on and on.

Option 3: Confess the Hurt

Confess is a theological term that means "to agree with." When the Bible talks about confessing sin, it means that we agree with God about our behavior. We don't excuse or rationalize or ignore what we have done. We honestly confess it.

Confessing our hurts is the first step in dealing with the pain others cause us. It means that we are completely honest about what happened and how we feel. We don't ignore it and we don't blow up and hurt others. Sometimes the best way to begin confessing is by writing down two key elements. First write what happened—the circumstances that triggered the hurt. Second, write your feelings about what happened.

Once you have written your personal confession of what happened and how you feel, you are ready to deal with the next step, forgiveness.

FORGIVENESS IS THE ACT OF LETTING GO OF THE PAST

Charles Stanley defines forgiveness as "the act of setting someone free from an obligation to you that is the result of a wrong done against you."[3]

Forgiveness has three elements. First, there is the reality of a wrong—someone has wronged you. Second, forgiveness includes a sense of obligation—the person who wronged you owes you something, at least an apology. Third, forgiveness is the act of releasing that person from the obligation—you cancel his or her debt.

In the original Greek of the New Testament the word for forgiveness is *aphiemi*. It means to send away or put apart. Although the word is used primarily for the concept of forgiveness, it is also used in a few other settings that give additional insight into the idea of forgiveness. *Aphiemi* is used as a technical term to describe divorce, as in "A husband must not divorce [*aphiemi*] his wife" (1 Cor. 7:11). When a divorce was granted during the first century, the people were immediately free from the obligations of marriage; the contract (marriage license) was canceled. *Aphiemi* is also used to describe leaving people behind, as in "He left [*aphiemi*] the crowd and went into the house" (Matt. 13:36). Another use of the word conveys the idea of releasing people after arrest. During the early days of the church, the apostles were arrested and brought before the religious leaders. One of the council members who was judging the apostles encouraged authorities to set them free. "Therefore, in the present case I advise you: Leave these men alone! Let them go [*aphiemi*]!" (Acts 5:38).

When we merge these various uses of *aphiemi* we get a general pattern of the substantive nature of forgiveness. Forgiveness means to cancel a legal obligation, to leave people behind and go on, to release prisoners from arrest. What is forgiveness? Forgiveness is canceling a legitimate obligation that is due you because of what another person has done. It is leaving that hurt behind and going on.

THE CPR OF FORGIVENESS

Understanding forgiveness is one thing; doing it is an entirely different matter. As philosopher C. S. Lewis said, "Everybody says forgiveness is a lovely idea until they have something to forgive."[4] How do you move from definition (understanding forgiveness) to application (practicing forgiveness)? Making this transition requires your personal initiative. Forgiveness begins with you even though it ought to begin with the other person. Seldom will the person who offended you come to you and ask your forgiveness, so you must take the first step. Jesus reinforced this idea in his teaching: "Therefore, if you are offering your gift at the altar and there remember that your brother has something against you, leave your gift there in front of the altar. First go and be reconciled to your brother; then come and offer your gift" (Matt. 5:23–24).

Notice carefully the teaching of Jesus. He is in effect saying, "When you come to worship God, you must not come if you are carrying a hurt that is the result of what someone else has done." Jesus instructs with a series of verbs. *Leave* your gift. *Go. Be reconciled.* Then *come* and *offer* your gift. Why must you take the first step when others have offended you? For two reasons. First, the other person may not even be aware that he or she has hurt you. Second, you must release the person so that your spiritual health will not be damaged.

So how do you go about forgiving? Let me suggest what I call the CPR of forgiveness.

C Stands for Confess

Confessing is the first step. Rather than ignoring your hurt, you must be honest about what happened and how you feel—yet without blowing up at the offender. As suggested above, a good way to confess the hurt is to write down what caused it and how you feel about it. Be honest and thorough.

P Stands for Pray

Forgiveness is not natural; it is supernatural. We would rather get revenge or at least get even, so forgiving another person cuts across our natural instincts. In fact, we cannot forgive unless we are empowered by God. *P* stands for pray. Pray for yourself, asking God to help you release the offender from the debt he or she owes you. Ask God to give you the courage to let go, to leave the hurt behind and go on. Pray also for the person who hurt you, asking God to help that person to be open to what you say and to be reconciled to you. Ask God to help you let that person go even if he or she rejects you further.

R Stands for Release

After you have confessed your hurt in writing and have prayed for yourself and for the one who hurt you, you must forgive that person by releasing him or her. Whenever possible, this should be done in person. Ask the individual to meet with you. Tell him or her that what you are about to say is very painful. Then read your written confession aloud and ask your offender to forgive you for the bad feelings you have had against him or her. Then tell the person that God is empowering you to forgive. When you get home, tear up your written confession and destroy it. This is your personal act of forgiving and letting go.

A CASE STUDY IN FORGIVENESS

For Johnny Carson fans and comedy channel addicts, Louis Anderson is no stranger. He is one of American's funniest comedians. Much of his material centers around the struggles of family life.

On Stage, Summerfest—Milwaukee, 1987

My dad never hit us . . . he carried a gun. Oh, he never shot us . . . he'd just go "Click-click!" Dads are funny, especially when they're driving. My dad would be riding down the middle of the street with me and my brother Tommy in the backseat. If he saw someone walking down the sidewalk who was a little different, he'd slow that car down, cock his head to the side, lean back, and scowl, "Looook at that, for cryin' out loud . . . get my rifle."

My favorite thing was when my dad would say stuff that made no sense. Like when he was trapped in traffic behind someone who was waiting to turn. "If I was the last person on earth," he'd say, "some moron would turn left in front of me!"

Underneath Anderson's humor is a pained and troubled childhood in a dysfunctional family with an alcoholic father. His book *Dear Dad* is his attempt to face his troubled childhood honestly and work through the pain in order to get to love and forgiveness. The book contains a series of letters written to his deceased dad. As part of a large and poor family, Louis grew up in constant fear of and with anger toward his drunken and abusive father. He writes extensively about these formative years.

I can remember coming home from school and knowing when I walked in the door whether or not you had been drinking—without even seeing anyone. That's how sensitive I think I became. I could just tell by instinct when you had been drinking. When you drank at night you'd sit in the room right next to the kitchen, and every time you sipped, the back of your head would tilt back around the corner. We'd see your head bob up and down like a cork floating in the pool. . . .

We all knew that night was going to get really bad when you downed the last beer and then pulled out a gallon

of wine. The stress on us was enormous. Exhausted after one
of these evenings, I would fall into bed, only to be woken up
a few hours later by a voice loud enough to rattle windows.
You'd be calling Mom a whore. Lots of times then, you'd
open my door, flick on the light, and yell, "Hey, lard ———— ,
when you going to lose some weight?"[5]

Louis continues to write about how these experiences had long-
term impact on the entire family.

I don't think you loved me. Maybe you did, but I never
felt it. I wonder how the rest of the family felt? No one talks
about it, but your drinking did affect us. Roger, Rhea, Jim,
Bill, Shanna, they all drank. I did, too, for a while. But, Dad,
your problem became my problem, all our problem.[6]

I have a hard time relating to what Louie went through. I had
the benefit of growing up in a healthy home where I was loved and
supported. But over the years I have prayed and cried with many
Louies—people whose adult lives are destroyed because of their
parents' influence. People who were abused verbally, physically,
religiously, sexually. People who lived in fear of what would happen next. People who never knew love and affection. And for
these people the present is hell and the prospect of the future is
worse because they are bound by the past.

The most gripping letter in Louis Anderson's book is the last
one. I have read it many times, and its power has gripped me each
time. It's the story of a visit to his dad's grave. When he gets to the
grave he puts his dad's black corduroy cap at the end of the grave-
stone. He then takes out a tape recorder with two sets of earphones
and puts one set of earphones on the headstone. He listens to the
tape recorder with the other set. Earlier he had recorded all of his
letters, and now he listens to all of them again—at the grave.

Louis then takes out some old photographs he has brought
with him.

This last picture is a close-up of you. There is a cigarette in your mouth, and you're wearing the same hat and
glasses that I have on now. I see the look on your face, in
your eyes, and you're looking directly at me, and I hear you
say, "I love you, Louie."

I know, Dad.

I forgive you. I understand.

I realize why I have come here and what I've been
looking for all this time. I wanted to be with you. And now I
am and always will be.

Oh yes. There's one more thing that I haven't said but
want to. And that one thing is, I love you.

Your son,
Louie

Louie finally does what he set out to do. He forgives his dad. He
finishes with the most difficult words of all—"I love you."

FORGIVENESS IS NEVER EASY

While the CPR of forgiveness is relatively easy to understand, it is *never* easy to do, because every situation is different
and every person is different. When you seriously pursue forgiving a parent, you discover how many obstacles can stand in the
way. One woman wrote me the following letter during a series of
talks I was giving on forgiveness.

When I heard about the subject matter for the next few
Saturday nights I became concerned. You see, too often the
subject of forgiveness is skimmed over and we tend to stick
to traditionally "safe" ground. I believe that there are many
like myself who bear wounds that run so deep that we are
unable to speak of these things in church (or in prayer), let
alone manage to forgive. In my case, I was sexually abused
by my father (a minister) during my preschool years. I lived
through subsequent years of physical and emotional abuse.

I recently confronted my father about the abuse (I'm now thirty-five years old).

He denies that it ever happened and refuses any responsibility. I am troubled with how to forgive someone who is unrepentant. I have never heard this subject addressed, and at times I feel like a failure as a Christian because I can't forgive this. I know that there must be others like myself who have heartaches that only the Lord can heal, so please consider carefully how deep some hurts run. I would hate to think that someone who was unsaved would not hear what he needs to hear at Calvary.

I'm going to pray that the Lord will give you insight and courage to address this delicate subject boldly. I believe at some point God will use this adversity in my life to allow me to help others who have suffered as I have.

Sincerely,
Your sister in Christ

In dealing with the complex issues that accompany forgiveness, there are several key factors to keep in mind.

1. *Forgiveness does not guarantee that the other person will change.* How can you forgive a father when he says he's sorry and will never again do the things that hurt you, yet he hurts you again and again?

Look at it this way: Forgiveness is something you do for your own benefit, not necessarily for the benefit of the person who hurt you. Sometimes in the aftermath of the courageous act of forgiveness a relationship is restored and the behavior of the offender is dramatically altered. However, this is not always the case. Remember that forgiveness is the act of letting that person go. If the person rejects your forgiveness, you may need to avoid that relationship as much as possible. Someone once asked me, "Can you forgive your parents—but still not want them in your life? If so, have you really forgiven them?" The answer to both questions is yes!

2. *Forgiveness does not mean immediate healing for your own life.* When a person is emotionally abused by a parent and brought up to feel worthless and unloved, how can that person overcome a negative self-image and feel worthy of God's love?

Forgiveness is not an antibiotic for everything that ails you. It is only the first step in rebuilding a broken life. Wounds that come from parents and others take time to heal. Sometimes professional counseling is necessary. It takes time to rebuild self-esteem and to stabilize trust. You can forgive an offender yet still struggle with your self-esteem. You can forgive someone yet still not trust that person. One girl wrote me:

> I am a fifteen-year-old girl, and I was raised with a very rough childhood. When I was four, my mother and I found my father dead on our living room floor. He committed suicide. Since my mom was only twenty, she didn't know how to handle things, and she began blaming me and physically abusing me. She even kicked me out of the house and sent me to my aunt's who was very much into satanism, so naturally I became satanic and had no idea of Christianity, until about six months ago when I went to a Christian youth home. I am still there, and I'm learning and getting out of satanism. I want to forgive my mom, but it's very hard. We are now starting to get along; and even though she doesn't hit me anymore, I am still scared she will at some point. Is this wrong?

It's not wrong to feel the fear that flows out of the nightmare of the past. While you must forgive, it may take time to work through all the damaged feelings that result from parental abuse.

3. *Forgiveness is both an act and a process.* The courageous act of releasing the person who hurt you is the beginning of forgiveness. You must guard against once again taking up the hurt. Something may remind you of what the person did, and all the feelings of hate and anger will come flooding back into your memory. If that happens, you must let go again. One person wrote, "I made the

decision to let go of my real dad, but as soon as he comes to visit, as soon as I see him, all the old feelings come back. How can I in a loving way tell him to stay out of my life?" Sometimes it is not possible for the person to stay out of your life. In this case, you must learn to keep releasing and forgiving.

CONCLUSION

If you have ever been to a circus, you may have seen an elephant confined by a rope tied around one leg and the other end attached to a stake in the ground. The elephant has more than enough power to break free, but instead it patiently stands there. The reason is that when a circus elephant is very young, it is confined in this way and, being young, it is unable to break free. So it gives up trying. Later on, when the elephant is older and bigger with the strength to break the bonds, it doesn't even try. It is tied to the image and memories of the past.

There are many people in similar circumstances. They are enslaved to the past. Forgiveness is a courageous act of breaking the rope and finding freedom.

♦

Chapter 5

COMING TO TERMS WITH WHO YOU ARE

♦

Therapists say that a positive self-image is one of the most—if not the most—vital ingredients for a healthy emotional life. It not only affects how we look and feel about ourselves, it also helps determine how well we relate to others, including those closest to us, and how successful we are in work and marriage. Many people live without a positive image of themselves. They don't like who they are and feel that their lives are not acceptable or valuable to others or to God.

Our self-image is developed primarily through the messages we receive from others, especially from our family of origin. The messages we are given as children usually stay with us when we are adults. If the messages are continually negative, then a person will likely grow up with a negative self-image. Some of the messages may be subtle, such as "Big boys don't cry." Some boys grow up with a garbage dump full of anger, hurt, and bitterness. Other messages are more direct: "You're stupid." "You're clumsy." "You're ugly." You're fat." "Why can't you be like your sister?" A steady diet of negative messages dooms people to lives filled with feelings of inadequacy. Dorothy Briggs, in her book *Celebrate Yourself*, gives a list of parents' most frequently enacted negative behaviors.

1. They overcontrolled.
2. Their demands were impossible for you to meet.
3. They imposed overly strict "should's," "ought's," "must's" "have to's," "can'ts."
4. They focused on what was wrong and missing.
5. They taught, "You are what you do"; your personal worth went down the drain with each misstep.
6. They were basically "against" you in that they had little faith in you.
7. They taught you to look to *others* to control you.
8. They taught you to disregard your intuitiveness and some or all of your feelings.[1]

When a poor self-image is imbedded in children, they compensate when they get to adulthood. They begin playing games or assuming roles and masks that keep others at a distance and prevent others from seeing their inner core. They may become perfectionists or workaholics. They may cover up their poor self-image with popular clothes, cars, hairstyles or drugs. They may become loners, cynics, critics, comics, or the ultimate people-pleasers. Many such people become outwardly successful, but this does not compensate for their inner pain. Whatever the games, the common denominator is that they are trying to find inner value and to feel good about themselves.

RECOGNIZING OUR REAL VALUE

The problem with trying to find self-worth in what we do, what we have, or what we accomplish is that it adds layers of clutter to our lives. We lack honesty and integrity. We are afraid of who we are. We are afraid that others will pull off our masks and walk away in disgust. We are afraid to face the truth about ourselves.

Much has been written in popular psychology about the games we play and about our need to cultivate healthy relationships. Yet not much has been written from a theological perspective. The message of psychology is that we should feel good about ourselves. The message that many theologians put forth is that we should feel bad about ourselves—after all, we are sinners. Actually, the Bible suggests two apparently contradictory objectives. First, we are to love our neighbors as ourselves (Luke 10:27). Second, unless we hate our parents, spouses, children, and even our "own life," we cannot be Jesus' disciples (Luke 14:26). As sinners, we are not worthy of heaven. But we are not worthless. A healthy self-image begins with a biblical understanding of who we are. Below are some foundational principles that affirm our worth as human beings.

We Are Valuable Because We Are Made in the Image of God

Then God said, "Let us make man in our image, in our likeness, and let them rule over the fish of the sea and the birds of the air, over the livestock, over all the earth, and over all the creatures that move along the ground" (Gen. 1:26). *Image* refers to the form or shape of something. *Likeness* describes similarity. We are both shaped in the form of God and similar to him. We reflect his characteristics. But we are not God; we are distinct from him. According to popular New Age thinking, we are all "gods." In fact, everything is "god"—trees, flowers, water, air, humans, animals, and so on. The Bible does not support this idea. In fact, such an idea is theological heresy and elevates the creation to the level of the Creator. But we do have significant value that is rooted in the reality that we reflect the One who created us—God. In what ways do we reflect the Creator?

1. *Perfection.* Adam and Eve were created perfect, and God declared them "very good." They had a perfect relationship with

God, with each other, and with their environment. They were righteous, holy, and without sin. But when they sinned they lost their perfection and were driven from paradise. Since then no human being has perfectly reflected God's image.

But Jesus came into the world to restore God's image in humans. As Christians we have "put on the new self, which is being renewed in knowledge in the image of [the] Creator" (Col. 3:10). One day this perfection will be completed when "we shall be like him, for we shall see him as he is" (1 John 3:2).

2. *Personality*. The second way we reflect God is through our personality. We are not animals who live by natural instinct, nor are we preprogrammed robots. We are human beings with minds that permit us to think, reason, create, and solve; with emotions that allow us to love, hate, laugh, and cry; and with wills that give us freedom to make choices. Our personalities set us apart from the rest of creation and reflect God, who likewise has a mind, emotions, and will.

3. *Spirituality*. The third way we reflect God's image is through our capacity to respond to him. Every human being has an innate knowledge of God (Rom. 1:20) and is on a journey to know him. Each of us is incomplete until we find God.

4. *Immortality*. We reflect God's image in that we were created to live forever. The Bible says that we are "destined to die once, and after that to face judgment" (Heb. 9:27). Our soul will live on forever.

We are valuable because we were created to reflect God's characteristics. We are not a higher form of animal; we are just a little lower than the angels (see Ps. 8). Nor are we the product of a lengthy process of natural selection. Rather, we are image-bearers of God.

We Are Valuable Because God Has Given Us Life

"The LORD God formed the man from the dust of the ground and breathed into his nostrils the breath of life, and the man became a living being" (Gen. 2:7). Let's take a close look at this verse. First we'll examine the verb "formed." It is the Hebrew word *yasar,* and it means to make something by design. It is used to describe the relationship of the potter to the clay (Jer. 18:2–4). The potter has a specific design for what he is making, and he deliberately shapes it to fulfill his purpose. So it is with God. When God created Adam, and by implication each of us, he did so with deliberate and purposeful intent.

Now let's look at the word "dust," or "clay." Both are the Hebrew word *adama,* from which "Adam" is derived. It describes the earthly and temporal nature of our physical bodies. We were molded like clay (Job 10:9), we live in houses of clay (Job 4:19), and one day we will return to the dust (Gen. 3:19).

Finally, let's see what is meant by "the breath of life." This phrase is never used with reference to animals but is used only when referring to God. The life that makes us fully human is a gift from God. Life should never be taken lightly or mistreated, because it comes from the Creator. It is his breath. Therefore, you are valuable. You are here by the design of God. And although your body will return to dust, the life you enjoy is a direct gift from God.

We Are Valuable Because We Exist by the Divine Purpose of God

No human being is a "mistake" or an "accident." We exist within the plan and purpose of a loving God. God had a purpose for our lives before we were even conceived. In referring to the prophet Jeremiah, God said:

> *Before I formed you in the womb I knew you,*
> *before you were born I set you apart;*
> *I appointed you as a prophet to the nations.*
>
> *(Jer. 1:5)*

God was active in accomplishing his purpose before we were born.

> *For you created my inmost being;*
>   *you knit me together in my mother's womb.*
> *I praise you because I am fearfully and wonderfully made;*
>   *your works are wonderful,*
>   *I know that full well.*
> *My frame was not hidden from you*
>   *when I was made in the secret place.*
> *When I was woven together in the depths of the earth,*
>   *your eyes saw my unformed body.*
> *All the days ordained for me*
>   *were written in your book*
>   *before one of them came to be.*
>
> *(Ps. 139:13–16)*

God's purpose for our lives predated our conception, and he is still interested in fulfilling his plans for us today.

We Are Valuable Because We Will Die According to the Purpose of God

The subject of death is usually avoided in social interaction. We prefer not to talk about it, yet it is an unavoidable reality. I conducted four funerals in the last two weeks. The first was the funeral of a forty-one-year-old husband who died after a four-year battle with cancer. The second was for a forty-three-year-old wife who was killed in an accident. She and her husband had stopped to help some friends who were involved in a minor accident. They crossed the street together and were standing on the shoulder of the highway when an oncoming truck swerved to miss the accident and hit her. She died instantly. The third funeral was that of an eighty-eight-year-old woman who had a long and prosperous life. The fourth was for a sixty-two-year-old man who only three weeks before his death was in the drama cast of our church's annual Christmas program. He was not feeling well and was admitted to the hospital. After extensive tests he was diagnosed with cancer, and one week later he died.

As I met, talked, and prayed with the families of the deceased I was reminded that God accomplishes his purpose even in death— even in the way we die. There are no accidents with God. While this does not excuse human responsibility, it nevertheless reminds us that even in death God is present and at work. Even our death has value. The Bible reassures us of God's purpose.

1. *We all will die—it's only a matter of when and how.*

The length of our days is seventy years—
  or eighty, if we have the strength;
yet their span is but trouble and sorrow,
  for they quickly pass, and we fly away.

(Ps. 90:10)

Not many people live past eighty—but some do. No one, however, can escape death. Technically, we all are dying now.

2. *God is involved with the time of our death.* After Christ's resurrection and shortly before his ascension, he met with his disciples for breakfast. He challenged the love of Peter. "Do you love me?" he asked three times (see John 21:15–17). Christ also predicted that Peter would live a long life and indicated "the kind of death by which Peter would glorify God" (v. 19). Jesus said, "When you are old you will stretch out your hands, and someone else will dress you and lead you where you do not want to go" (v. 18). Peter then wanted to know about John's future. Jesus told him, "If I want him to remain alive until I return, what is that to you?" (v. 22). Jesus was saying that Peter's life and John's life were up to God. Whatever Jesus wanted would happen.

3. *We can shorten or extend our days.* The Bible teaches that we can shorten our lives through destructive and sinful choices.

Paul reminded the church at Corinth that some of their members were sick and some died prematurely because of their sin in disregarding the sacred nature of the Lord's Supper (1 Cor. 11:29–30). We can shorten our lives by sinful disregard of God or blatant disregard of the laws of health.

The Bible gives at least one story where God extended someone's life beyond what was originally set. God told Hezekiah, "Put your house in order, because you are going to die; you will not recover" (2 Kings 20:1). Hezekiah poured out his heart to God in prayer, and God responded by extending Hezekiah's life another fifteen years (2 Kings 20:6). This story gives me hope when I pray for people who appear to be dying. Sometimes God chooses to extend our days in answer to prayer.

We know that we are valuable, because from before our conception and until death and beyond, God is present with us and is accomplishing his purpose for our lives.

We Are Valuable Because of Our Relationship With God

While it is true that a healthy self-image is vital for emotional health, I do not believe that a positive self-image is our number one need. Our number one need is to have a proper relationship with God and to discover who we are in him. The biblical realities of our relationship with God form a solid foundation for a healthy, spiritual self-image. Consider the following:

1. *God loves us unconditionally.* God's love does not come with preconditions. He does not say, "I love you, *but* . . . ." Rather, he says, "I love you—period."

God loved us when we were sinners and separated from him. Paul wrote, "God demonstrates his own love for us in this: While we were still sinners, Christ died for us" (Rom. 5:8). We do not have to work to earn God's love; he loves us as we are—with all our imperfections, dysfunctions, and sin. There is nothing we can do to make God love us more and nothing we can do to make him love us less.

2. *God forgives all our sin.* "In [Christ] we have redemption, the forgiveness of sins" (Col. 1:14). What a wonderful blessing. When I was younger we sang an old gospel song:

> *Rolled away, rolled away, rolled away.*
> *Every burden of my heart rolled away.*
> *Every sin had to go, 'neath the crimson flow.*
> *Rolled away, rolled away, rolled away.*
> *Every burden of my heart rolled away.*

To be forgiven is to be liberated from the past and relieved of the guilt we bear and the regrets we carry. It is to be given a new beginning, to be liberated from the past.

3. *God accepts us into his family.* John assured his readers, "To all who received him, to those who believed in his name, he gave the right to become children of God" (John 1:12). And Paul prayed that the Colossians would "[give] thanks to the Father, who has qualified you to share in the inheritance of the saints in the kingdom of light. For he has rescued us from the dominion of darkness and brought us into the kingdom of the Son he loves" (Col. 1:12–13).

When we become part of the family of God we are both rescued from darkness and given citizenship in the kingdom of light. Several months ago I traveled to Alma Ata, Kazakhstan. I left Grand Rapids on a Sunday night and flew through the night to Paris, France. I had a five-hour layover in Paris and then boarded a second flight to fly through the second night to Kazakhstan. After flying through eleven time zones and two nights, I arrived in the predawn darkness of Tuesday morning. I did not know who would meet me. After getting through customs, I saw a tall Russian man holding a cardboard sign with my name on it. I introduced myself, and a young man next to the Russian holding the sign responded in beautiful English. "We welcome you in the love of Jesus." As I rode in a van through the streets of a foreign city with two people I had never met before, I was thankful to be part of God's family. I was not with strangers. I was with brothers—family.

4. *God changes us into new people.* "Therefore, if anyone is in Christ, he is a new creation; the old has gone, the new has come!" (2 Cor. 5:17).

Time and space would not permit me to tell the story of changed lives in our church. Drug addicts, prostitutes, gossips, homosexuals, liars, alcoholics, cheaters, etc., etc., etc. When the Spirit brought conviction to their lives and they repented of their sins and turned to faith in Christ, God changed their lives. He gave them a new beginning with new desires, new perspectives, new relationships, and a new self-image (see Rom. 8:28–29). What he did for them, he did for me as well.

5. *God keeps us in his love.*

> Who shall separate us form the love of Christ? Shall trouble or hardship or persecution or famine or nakedness or danger or sword? As it is written:

> "For your sake we face death all day long;
>   we are considered as sheep to be slaughtered."

> No, in all these things we are more than conquerors through him who loved us. For I am convinced that neither death nor life, neither angels nor demons, neither the present nor the future, nor any powers, neither height nor depth, nor anything else in all creation, will be able to separate us from the love of God that is in Christ Jesus our Lord. (Rom. 8:35–39)

This is one of my favorite passages of Scripture. I almost always read this passage and comment on it at the funeral of believers. It speaks of the security of God's love. *Nothing* can ever sever us from his love. Look at the list:

- Not death nor life
- Not angels nor demons

- Not the present nor the future
- Not any powers
- Not height nor depth

What a list! None of these things can remove us from God's love. For fear of leaving anything out, Paul adds, "nor anything else in all creation" (Rom. 8:39). I have value because I am secure in the love of Christ and nothing in this world or the world to come can change this reality.

TO WHOM ARE YOU GOING TO LISTEN?

If you have been listening to and believing messages that have caused you to have a negative self-image, it is time for you to start listening to what God has to say about you. What does God say?

You are valuable because you are made in my image.
You are valuable because I gave you life.
You are valuable because you are part of my purpose
      and plan.
You are valuable because I am present with you in life and
      in death.
You are valuable because I love you unconditionally.
You are valuable because I have forgiven you.
You are valuable because you are part of my family.
You are valuable because I have given you a new
      beginning.
You are valuable because you are forever safe in my love.

Play these messages over and over again until you start to believe them. And whether you believe them fully or not, they are still true. You matter to God and should therefore matter to yourself.

◆

Chapter 6

TAKING CARE OF YOURSELF

◆

Life is often like a treadmill—you can't slow it down and you can't get off. And besides that, it seems that it keeps going faster and faster. It was during one of these hectic times in my life that I decided to discuss the pace of my life and ministry with our church board. They listened sympathetically and offered many helpful suggestions for slowing down. They talked about maintaining a regular day off, taking periodic study breaks, and delegating responsibilities.

After a lengthy discussion one of the elders spoke up. "Ed," he said, "this board really has no guts, and you need to know it. We will tell you what you should do and not do. Then we will go home tonight feeling good that we are protecting you. The truth is that we will cheer you into your grave, bury you, and find another pastor. The only person who will take care of you is you!" Blunt advice and good advice: "The only person who will take care of you is you." You can develop an accountability group, attend time-management seminars, and set goals, but the *only* person who will take care of you is you. I have discovered that three main areas of taking care of myself require continued vigilance—resting regularly, eating properly, and exercising consistently.

A SABBATH REST

> Remember the Sabbath day by keeping it holy. Six days you shall labor and do all your work, but the seventh day is a Sabbath to the LORD your God. On it you shall not do any work, neither you, nor your son or daughter, nor your manservant or maidservant, nor your animals, nor the alien within your gates. For in six days the LORD made the heavens and the earth, the sea, and all that is in them, but he rested on the seventh day. Therefore the LORD blessed the Sabbath day and made it holy. (Ex. 20:8–11)

When I was growing up our family practiced "sabbath regulations" on Sunday. We could not play with our friends, watch television, or do homework. We went to church, ate together, rested, and read the Bible. All other activities were taboo. This was my parents' way of observing a sabbath rest. Of course the danger with this approach is that one can focus on what one cannot do rather then enjoying the original purpose of the sabbath.

The sabbath was given by God and was intended to be a time of joyful celebration. The instructions were clear. "Six days you shall labor and do all your work, but the seventh day is a Sabbath to the LORD your God. On it you shall not do any work" (Ex. 20:9–10). The word *sabbath* means "rest." It carries the idea of a complete time-out from the routine of daily work. It was a rest for family, employees, animals, and foreigners. And for the people who lived and worked in ancient cultures, this rest was a welcome and joyful blessing.

Consider the farmers. They worked without the assistance of tractors, combines, and other modern machinery. They cleared the rocks, tilled the soil, hoed, watered, and harvested all by hand. This was back-breaking, exhausting work under the heat of the sun. Thus Sunday was a welcome relief. Consider the carpenters. They worked without the benefit of lumber yards, power tools, and pick-up trucks. Consider mothers. They baked, cooked, and washed without electric ranges, microwaves, refrigerators, vacuum cleaners, and running water. For mothers, the sabbath was more than a welcome relief—it was a day of rest and renewal.

The sabbath was a gift from God for his people's benefit. By New Testament times the rabbis had added fifteen hundred laws to define what one could and could not do on the sabbath. They wrote twenty-four chapters of detailed guidelines and identified thirty-nine kinds of work that were prohibited. By the time of Jesus the observance of the sabbath was oppressive—certainly not God's intent. In fact, Jesus said that the "Sabbath was made for man, not man for the Sabbath" (Mark 2:27). Psalm 92 is devoted to the meaning of the sabbath, and it is a psalm of incredible celebration and joy.

> *It is good to praise the LORD*
> *and make music to your name, O Most High,*
> *to proclaim your love in the morning*
> *and your faithfulness at night,*
> *to the music of the ten-stringed lyre*
> *and the melody of the harp.*
>
> *For you make me glad by your deeds, O LORD;*
> *I sing for joy at the works of your hands.*
>
> *(vv. 1–4)*

The Sabbath: A Time to Refocus

God created the world in six days, and on the seventh he rested. He did not rest because he was tired. After all, he is God.

He rested to establish a pattern for us—a pattern of rest that promotes personal renewal. As human beings we cannot work without rest and without taking a day off. Failure to conform to this cycle of work and rest fosters burnout. The original instructions for the sabbath included prohibitions against gathering food, going out of the home, and working (Ex. 16:29–30). The sabbath was given for physical, emotional, and spiritual renewal. It is also a time for giving attention to God, oneself, and one's family.

1. *A time to pay attention to God.* According to Exodus 20:10, the seventh day was to be "a Sabbath to the LORD your God." It was not just a day off; it was to be directed to God. It provided a time when people could refocus their priorities by paying attention to God.

Certain dimensions of God's character were associated with the sabbath, one of which was *Creator.* "For in six days the LORD made the heavens and the earth, the sea, and all that is in them, but he rested on the seventh day. Therefore the LORD blessed the Sabbath day and made it holy" (Ex. 20:11). The sabbath was a reminder of God's creative work, a time to recognize God as the creator and sustainer of the universe. It was a reminder that human beings are not in control—God is! As people worked from morning to night on the first six days of the week, it would be easy for them to assume that they were in control of their own destiny. But on the sabbath they rested and reflected on God being in control. We observe a day of rest to affirm our belief that God is our Creator and that he is in control. He is our source (Gen. 14:21–24) and our strength (Isa. 40:28–31).

Another characteristic of God associated with the sabbath was *Redeemer.* In Deuteronomy, where the Ten Commandments are repeated, an additional reason is given for keeping the sabbath: "Remember that you were slaves in Egypt and that the LORD your God brought you out of there with a mighty hand and an outstretched arm. Therefore the LORD your God has commanded you to observe the Sabbath day" (5:15). Two lessons can be learned from this statement. First, there is a spiritual lesson. Egypt represents our sinful condition before we met Christ. God delivered us from slavery to sin through the blood of Jesus Christ, our Passover Lamb. The sabbath is an opportunity to thank God for his redemptive work through Jesus Christ.

The second lesson is a literal one. The children of Israel were "slaves" for four hundred years, and thus they had no "days off " or "Sabbaths" for four centuries. Once God had delivered them, they were to observe the sabbath and reflect on the goodness and power of God who had set them free. The compelling lesson for us is that we too can become slaves to work—workaholics. We don't take time off for a sabbath. In our addiction we lose our direction, our Godward perspective. One way to combat our tendency toward voluntary slavery to work is to take one day a week off from all work and focus our attention on the God who sets us free from *all* addictions.

A third attribute of God to which we need to pay attention is as *the giver of eternal life*. The sabbath rest is connected to the reality of eternal rest. "Since the promise of entering his rest still stands, let us be careful that none of you be found to have fallen short of it. . . . There remains, then, a Sabbath-rest for the people of God" (Heb. 4:1–9).

Part of sabbath observance is to remember what God has done in the past—God as Creator and Redeemer. But another part of sabbath observance is to look to the future. Whenever I remember the sabbath, I am also looking forward to the reality of heaven and the eternal sabbath-rest. The earthly sabbath is a small reminder that we are heaven bound.

Since part of the purpose of keeping the sabbath is to pay attention to God as Creator, Redeemer, and giver of eternal life, once a week we ought to review our past week to see how we lived in light of God's character. I recommend weekly reflection of the following questions:

1. If God is Creator and is in control, did I live this past week as if God was in control or as if I was in control?
2. If God sets us free from slavery, did I live this past week addicted to work (or to the phone, the fax, the E-mail, etc.)?
3. If God is leading us to eternity, what have I done this past week that will matter in eternity?

2. A time to pay attention to yourself. The sabbath is not only a time to pay attention to God, it is also a time to pay attention to yourself. In the Old Testament the principle of the sabbath was practiced in three ways.

First, there was the weekly sabbath, a day of *rest*. The second application was the sabbath year. "For six years sow your fields, and for six years prune your vineyards and gather their crops. But in the seventh year the land is to have a sabbath of rest, a sabbath to the LORD. Do not sow your field or prune your vineyards" (Lev. 25:3–4). The sabbath year offered *relief* for both the land and the people. Third, there was the Year of Jubilee (Lev. 25:8–55), a year of sabbath. Every fiftieth year slaves were freed, property was returned to its original owner, and the people rested. The key concept was *restoration.* So the three goals of the sabbath are rest, relief, and restoration.

Life is a physical, emotional, and spiritual drain. For six days we run, work, give, and fight. The sabbath is to be for *us* a day of rest, relief, and restoration. We are to be renewed physically, emotionally, and spiritually by taking a God-given time-out.

3. A time to pay attention to your family. God gave specific instructions that would force parents to pay attention to their families on the sabbath. "Bear in mind that the LORD has given you the Sabbath; that is why on the sixth day he gives you bread for two days. Everyone is to stay where he is on the seventh day; no one is to go out. So the people rested on the seventh day" (Ex. 16:29–30).

The people were to stay inside their tents with their families for the entire day. What did they do all day? There were no televisions or computer games, no newspapers or magazines, and no books or radios. What did they do? They ate. They slept. They talked. What a novel idea for building family intimacy! If ever there was a time when families needed to spend time together and reconnect, it is today. We need to "bond," and this was God's intent when he gave the principle of sabbath rest.

Rest, Relief, Restoration

Life was not meant to be lived with the tachometer in the red zone everyday. If we live this way, the engine will eventually blow up. God intended for us to take off at least one day from work to find rest, relief, and restoration—a time to pay attention to God, ourselves, and our families. Your day of rest may or may not be Sunday. Sunday is my most demanding work day, so my sabbath is Thursday—a day away from work and ministry. The following questions serve as a guide for observing the sabbath:

1. Do I have time to pay attention to God?
2. Is it restful? Do I find relief and restoration?
3. Is it helpful for my family? Do I spend time with them?
4. Is it a holy day? Is it different and distinct from the rest of the week?
5. Do I feel closer to God at the end of the day?
6. Am I more committed to my family at the end of the day?
7. Am I rested and ready to go for another week?

Taking care of yourself must include rest. It also includes paying attention to our diet.

YOU ARE WHAT YOU EAT

A number of years ago I spoke at a regional pastors' meeting. I was the substitute for one of the speakers who had resigned his church the previous week because of improper conduct. I had been at the church for the resignation, and so I was asked to speak to these pastors and explain what had happened to their colleague. As I discussed the events that led to his resignation, I mentioned that he had made some mistakes. When I used the word *mistake* a pastor spoke up from the crowd and said, "Call it what it is brother. Call it sin!" I looked over to see who had said this. It was a pastor who weighed at least 350 pounds and was grossly overweight. I agreed with him that it was sin. What I wanted to say, however, was "Gluttony is sin as well, brother." Later at lunch I watched this pastor eat unbelievably massive amounts of food. No wonder he was obese.

Part of me is cynical in regard to overweight people. The other part is sympathetic. Think of the excess weight they carry around and the stress it puts on their body. America is a country of overweight people. Until 1980, about 25 percent of Americans were overweight. During the 1980s this figure rose to more than 33 percent. Today more than 58 million Americans are at least 20 percent over their ideal body weight.[1] Americans are eating more, eating larger portions, eating between meals, and eating junk food. Their eating habits, coupled with little or no exercise, have produced our current dilemma.

Unfortunately, Christians are not immune from the dangers of overeating. But they should demonstrate the necessary control to avoid overindulgence. The Bible advises us to take radical action to avoid the *sin* of gluttony: "When you sit to dine with a ruler, note well what is before you, and put a knife to your throat if you are given to gluttony. Do not crave his delicacies, for that food is deceptive" (Prov. 23:1–3). Putting a knife to your throat is radical—but effective—action.

To begin a discussion on diet is to enter a never-ending debate. Actually, the scientific rules of diet are rather simple.

Godfrey Fowler, an Oxford University physician, summarized them well:

1. The main task is to avoid obesity. This is more the province of exercise. We are not overweight, we are overfat. Only exercise will give us muscle to replace that fat. When you exercise consistently your preoccupation with diet will disappear.
2. Average sugar intake should be halved. Cut down on candy, soft drinks, sugar in tea or coffee.
3. Fat should be reduced to about 30 percent of the diet. Cut down on butter, margarine, cream, fat on meats, and fried foods.
4. Increase intake of fiber. Use whole-grain cereals or, in a pinch, Metamucil.
5. Alcohol intake should be kept to two "units" a day (two pints of beer or glasses of wine).[2]

This is not a book about forming proper eating habits, but it is a reminder that disciplined eating is a vital ingredient for healthy living. Many problems would be solved if people would avoid junk food, eat less, and exercise regularly. (The temptation is to point specifically to obese people, but they are not the only ones with poor eating habits—others do also, but don't have the outward appearance of them.) Christians should be models of restraint and fitness.

EXERCISE

Diet and exercise are the two vital components of health. The American Dietetic Association recommends the following for weight control and exercise.

1. A nutritionally adequate diet and exercise are major contributing factors to physical fitness and health. The ADA

feels that there is substantial evidence that such a diet should avoid excess intake of calories, fat, cholesterol, sugar, salt, and highly refined foods lacking in fiber.

2. Weight loss and weight maintenance should be achieved by a combination of dietary modifications, change in eating behavior, and regular aerobic exercise.

3. Skin-fold measurements should be used to determine level of body fatness. Acceptable levels of body fat range from 7 to 15 percent for men and from 12 to 25 percent in women. However, with well-trained runners body fat is seldom higher than 6 percent in males and 12 percent in females.

4. The generally healthy individual who regularly consumes a diet that supplies the Recommended Dietary Allowances receives all the necessary nutrients for a physical conditioning program.

5. Intensity, duration, and frequency of exercise should be determined according to the age, physical condition, and health status of the individual.

6. The habits of a nutritionally balanced diet and physical fitness should be established during childhood and maintained throughout life.[3]

Running is my exercise of choice. For people who do not enjoy running, any exercise that promotes stamina, such as walking, swimming, or cycling, will do just as well. The minimum goal is to exercise at least three times a week for twenty minutes or more at a moderate pace (you should be able to talk while exercising). If you have been sedentary, start by getting a physical and exercising under a doctor's supervision. So why exercise, or in my case, why run?

I exercise for fitness. Because I played and coached soccer until I was thirty, I had little need for exercising to maintain fitness. During the season, I played daily in practice. In the off-season I played indoors. In the summer I taught coaching camps and clinics. I was in fine physical condition. But when I retired from coaching and found my fitness level retiring as well, I decided to run.

I never enjoyed running when I was playing soccer. Running was a chore, a painful and necessary prerequisite for being able to play at a high level of energy and intensity. Since running was always a means to an end, I was hesitant to run just to run. But as I began to adjust to running, I also began to enjoy it. I realized that running is a simple form of exercise that I can do without teammates or special equipment and skills. It keeps me fit and fits my schedule.

I have been running for more than fifteen years now and have gone through many phases, including a racing phase, during which I ran fifty to seventy-five miles a week, and a marathon and triathlon phase. Over the years I have achieved a sense of balance in my running. In the winter I try to run three or four miles three to four times a week. In the summer I run more— twenty to twenty-five miles a week. This moderate schedule keeps me at a good level of fitness.

I exercise for my mind. The second reason I run is to reduce stress and to unclutter my mind. After about a mile I begin to settle into my run. It is then that the stress starts to dissipate with the sweat running down my face. Breathing fresh air, being close to nature, seeing the clouds and the sun, and feeling the wind in my face all help me to relax. Somehow the pressures of life do not seem as critical as they did before I laced up my shoes.

Running is an opportunity to let my mind wander. There are no phones, no appointments, and no people, only my rhythmic breathing and the pounding of my feet against the pavement. I am alone with my thoughts. Sometimes I pray, meditate on Scripture, or go over my sermons when I run. Sometimes I ponder decisions I must make. And sometimes I don't think of anything in particular. Running refreshes my mind.

I exercise for fun. Running is my recreation, my hobby. I love to run in the snow and in the heat. I love to run on roads, in the woods, in the mountains, and on the beach. Some of my happiest and most enjoyable times have been out running.

I remember running from Lynchburg to Big Island (a logging town about twenty-three miles away) with my friend David Horton, a nationally ranked ultramarathoner (fifty- and one-hundred-mile races). We left the city and began down a country road at the foot of the Blue Ridge Mountains. We passed a sign that said, "Big Island, 10 miles." We had already run thirteen miles, but something seemed to say, "Go for it." As we descended down into Big Island we realized we had no money for drinks, so we started picking up returnable bottles so that we could get enough money for drinks. When we got to Big Island, we turned in the bottles but did not have enough for a drink—we bought Tootsie Rolls instead. Since there was no way we could run back home, I called my wife to ask her to pick us up. We sat down on the curb to wait, and it started to rain. There we were, dressed in our cute nylon shorts, no shirts, sitting in the rain on the curb in a town filled with loggers.

I remember racing to beat a severe thunderstorm in Kansas. The skies were black, the wind was gusting, and the lightning was flashing. Personal survival drove me. I remember running along a river on an old railroad bed. The fall colors were incredible. Then a deer ran across the track a few feet in front of me and scared me half to death. I remember running the beaches in the Bahamas, Miami, New Jersey, North Carolina, and California. I remember running in a park in Poland and along a trail on the cliffs next to the ocean in Ireland. But most of all I remember the daily runs in familiar territory—the three miles out and back and the four mile loop that have become my friends. They are the same and yet they are different every time I run them.

RULES FOR LIVING

No one will take care of you but you. Rest, diet, and exercise are your responsibility. Out of the Breslow research at UCLA[4] there developed seven rules for taking care of oneself.

1. Eat a good breakfast.
2. Don't eat between meals.
3. Maintain your weight.
4. Don't smoke.
5. Drink moderately [my rule is don't drink at all].
6. Get a good night's sleep.
7. Exercise regularly.

These rules sound so simple and they are. The difficulty is in living by them.

◆

Part 3

FINDING OUTWARD SIMPLICTY

◆

◆

Chapter 7

SIMPLE LOVE CAN COMPLICATE YOUR LIFE

◆

The envelope did not look significantly different from the envelopes of the dozens of letters I receive each week. But the contents soon altered the direction of my life and ministry. It was a letter from a former member of our church who had lost her husband, remarried, and moved to another city. The letter was about her son Jim.[1] Jim had grown up in our church and had been active in Sunday school and in the youth group. But when he turned eighteen he left the church for good. For many of his years in church he had struggled with his sexuality, and at age eighteen he left the Christian community and gravitated to the gay community. When I received the letter, Jim was thirty-five and hospitalized in serious condition. His mother feared that he had AIDS and asked if I would go and visit him.

Jim was not the first person I had known with HIV/AIDS. There was Michael, with whom I had traveled for an entire summer on an evangelistic team. Over the years I lost contact with him and someone told me that he had died with complications from the AIDS virus. And there was Sam, a hemophiliac whom I visited many times. He also died of complications from the virus.

I went to the hospital to visit Jim on a weekday evening. A sign on his door said to check with the nursing station before entering his room. I did and was given permission to enter. The room was dimly lit, and Jim was all alone. I introduced myself and told Jim that his mom had written me a letter and asked me to visit him. Jim did not say a lot.

I told him that his mom feared that he might have AIDS. He told me that the doctor was just in to see him and that his blood tests did indicate that he was HIV-positive. I was the first person he talked to since he received the news. I did not say a lot. I could tell he was afraid. I later found out that Jim thought he was going to die that night! I took his hand to offer a prayer, and it felt as if it was on fire; he had an extremely high fever. After praying, I left him Billy Graham's tract *Peace With God*.

When I went to see Jim the next day his fever had broken, and he was sitting up in bed. He had a smile on his face. "I read the booklet," he said, "and I invited Christ into my life." Soon Jim was released from the hospital and began a five-year war against the virus. Jim and I became friends, and Jim occasionally attended our church. One of the families in our church "adopted" him. They often had him over to eat, and they walked with him through his battle. He watched our church television program every week and often offered suggestions on how to improve it. We ate lunch together and talked about the loneliness of his battle against HIV and about the hatred and rejection of homosexuals and AIDS victims by many Christians.

The last time I was with Jim, a few days before he died, was in a hospital room—the place where our friendship had begun. AIDS had robbed his body of eyesight, health, and vitality. Two friends were with him, and we joined hands and prayed for Jim. I knew it would be my last prayer with him, and it was hard to find words. Even as I write I am overcome with emotion.

WHATEVER HAPPENED TO LOVE?

Every Christian would agree on the importance of love. Jesus made it clear that the greatest commandment is to love God, and the second greatest is to love your neighbor as yourself. But what if your neighbor is HIV-positive? What if your neighbor is gay? When it comes to HIV or homosexuality, it is very hard to find love in action within the Christian community.

It is not that Christians are unloving. We love alcoholics, drug addicts, prisoners, adulterers, and prostitutes. But gays or people who have HIV? The language we use in addressing this virus is radically different than the language we use in addressing other issues of sin and disease. When it comes to gays, the language is harsh: "They're nothing but perverts." "They're disgusting." "They deserve AIDS." "Faggots!" The language is little better when it comes to HIV, unless one has contracted HIV from a blood transfusion—then one is deeply loved and helped. But if HIV comes from drugs or sex, the person is under the judgment of God. "You deserve to get what you've got, and if you hadn't done what you did, you wouldn't have gotten what you've got!"

Are we not called upon to love everyone? After all, is this not the way God loves? Moreover, is not the test of our love a matter of loving the people who are the most difficult to love? It's easy to love the lovable, but to love the outcasts of society demands the highest experience of God's love. In fact, unless we are willing to love the "least," then we have not really loved at all. Jesus teaches that to love the least is to express our love to Christ himself.

"The King will reply, 'I tell you the truth, whatever you did for one of the least of these brothers of mine, you did for me.'

> "Then he will say to those on his left, 'Depart from me, you who are cursed, into the eternal fire prepared for the devil and his angels. For I was hungry and you gave me nothing to eat, I was thirsty and you gave me nothing to drink, I was a stranger and you did not invite me in, I needed clothes and you did not clothe me, I was sick and in prison and you did not look after me.'
>
> "They also will answer, 'Lord, when did we see you hungry or thirsty or a stranger or needing clothes or sick or in prison, and did not help you?'
>
> "He will reply, 'I tell you the truth, whatever you did not do for one of the least of these, you did not do for me.'" (Matt. 25:40–45)

"I was sick . . . and you did not look after me." These are haunting words. Frankly, I do not completely understand the theology of this passage. I do not know how taking care of the sick—including HIV-positive people—is equal to taking care of Jesus. I do not know how Jesus is uniquely present in the marginalized people mentioned in this passage. But not understanding the theology does not excuse my responsibility to practice compassion.

Love, however, does not mean the denial of truth. When it comes to HIV/AIDS there is one compelling truth—most of the transmissions of the disease can be prevented! The best way to prevent sexual transmission, for example, is to practice sex within the commitment of lifelong heterosexual marriage. This is in fact what the Bible teaches. People who practice sex outside these boundaries risk contracting sexually transmitted diseases including HIV/AIDS. This is the truth, but it does not exempt us from loving those who have ignored the truth and are suffering the consequences of bad choices.

The Bible's stand on homosexuality is clear: All sex outside of the lifelong commitment of heterosexual marriage is sin. Homosexuality is outside the boundaries of God's creative intent and clearly revealed will. But this truth does not give us the right to ignore every-one who has violated the Bible's teaching. The fact is, all of us are sinners in need of God's love, grace, and forgiveness.

FACING UP TO HIV/AIDS

My journey of love did not end with Jim. After listening to and crying with him over a period of months, I began to sense the need to lead our church into a more active role in regard to people with HIV/AIDS. One question haunted me: What would Jesus do? I became convinced that he would reach out to people with HIV/AIDS. After all, he touched and healed the lepers of his day who were social, religious, and cultural outcasts. They were con-sidered "unclean" and in many cases under the judgment of God—yet Jesus healed them. In many ways, people with HIV/AIDS are the lepers of today.

Our church's involvement was a progressive journey that involved many different factors. I invited Ed, a man with AIDS, to meet with the church board. I met Ed a few weeks after he accepted Christ. He had become a drug addict during military service in Vietnam and more recently had begun attending "Sat-urday Night"—our nontraditional, seeker-sensitive service—while also going through a drug rehabilitation program.

By the time Ed finished telling his story, the entire board was in tears. That led to the church's developing a policy on AIDS. It begins:

> It is the policy of Calvary Church to welcome people with AIDS in our public worship services, to accept them and extend to them the love and compassion of Christ.
>
> Participation in the educational programs of the church will be governed by the communicable disease guidelines which are available at the church office.

Our policy is a reminder that love must be expressed in prudent and wise ways. We cannot place other people at high risk to express love.

But we did not stop there. Our Christian commitment propelled us out into the community where people are suffering and dying. I tracked down the local AIDS Resource Center, which I found located in one of the worst neighborhoods of our city. As I walked in the door I was wondering if any people who recognized me saw me go in. If they did, maybe they would spread the word and assume that I had HIV or was gay. For about an hour the director talked to me about the center and the extent of the HIV problem in Grand Rapids. I discovered later that the director was shocked that the pastor of a conservative evangelical church had any interest in HIV/AIDS. The director gave me a list of people who were on the forefront of HIV/AIDS education and prevention and told me that I should talk with them before we did anything at all. On the list was the name of the pastor of the Metropolitan Community Church in Grand Rapids, a pro-gay church.

I called George, the pastor of that church, and told him that our church was interested in getting involved. He agreed to meet me and suggested that we meet at my office. "I've always wanted to see your building," he said.

The meeting lasted almost two hours. I don't know if George was nervous, but I was.

"Before we talk about HIV/AIDS," I said, "I want you to know that I am aware of your theological position on homosexuality. I assume you are aware of my position. I would prefer to set aside discussion on that issue, because I know that you would not change my mind and that I would not change your mind."

He smiled and said, "Okay," and the conversation began. I don't recall everything we talked about, but I do remember one thing George said. He told me that he had known more than sixty people who had already died with AIDS. I was overwhelmed with

this statistic. I kept looking into George's eyes trying to understand what it would be like to live through so many losses. I could
not get over the fact that I was talking with a fellow human being
who had lived in the trenches of rejection, disease, and death. I
felt great compassion for this man whom I had just met.

The outcome of the meeting was that George recommended
that we focus our efforts on families with AIDS. He felt that they
were the most neglected people in the HIV/AIDS community. He
felt that our theology of sexuality would prohibit significant ministry to the gay community, although he did not completely rule
out such ministry.

When most churches get involved in an issue like AIDS,
they usually start their own ministry. This was certainly an option
for us, but I felt that we should help those already involved,
including secular organizations. The purpose of the AIDS
Resource Center is to provide education, help, and prevention
resources to the community. It is not a religious organization, but
I knew that it was the appropriate place to begin our journey.

So how do we help? One of our church members serves on
the board of the AIDS Resource Center. For several years now we
have purchased Christmas presents for families affected by
HIV/AIDS. We also offer our chapel free of charge for funeral services and underwrite funeral expenses for those who die of
HIV/AIDS and do not have enough money for a funeral. These are
small steps in the right direction.

TELLING THE CHURCH

After the board had developed a policy on HIV/AIDS and
had decided to get involved in the community of suffering people,
it was time to inform the entire church of this new direction. In
the providence of God, we had a special speaker on Sunday morning. I knew of this man's concern for HIV-positive people and

asked him to address this issue. At the end of the sermon he told a gripping story about an elderly Christian leader in a small rural church who had contracted AIDS through a blood transfusion during surgery.

When people found out that the man had AIDS their relationship with him changed drastically. The pastor refused to visit him, and lifelong friends avoided him. He became a rejected and isolated man in a church he had faithfully served for years. At the end of this gripping story, the speaker revealed that this man who died with AIDS was his dad.

That morning I announced that our church would begin ministering to the HIV/AIDS community. I told about our policy and our desire to make a difference in Grand Rapids. Letters of objection came pouring in that week. One person wrote, "If you get involved with HIV/AIDS this church will be overrun with homosexuals." Another wrote, "You're just a homo lover." I felt impressed to address their criticism publicly, so on Sunday morning I quoted their criticisms and then said: "Yes, it is possible that we will be overrun with homosexuals. If the church gets overrun with homosexuals, that will be terrific. They can take their place in the pews right next to the liars, gossips, materialists, and all the rest of us who entertain sin in our lives." I concluded by saying, "When I die, if someone stands up and says, 'Ed Dobson loved homosexuals,' then I will have accomplished something with my life." When I finished, people applauded. It was an overwhelming moment of affirmation.

BE CAREFUL WHAT YOU SAY

Sometime later *Christianity Today* did an article on homosexuality. In the middle of the article was a section titled—in large, bold print—"Ed Dobson Loves Homosexuals."[2]

The article wasn't my idea. Frankly, I was not sure I wanted many people outside our community to know what we were doing, because it would generate a lot of misunderstanding and criticism among Christians. The media's making such a big deal about Christians loving homosexuals also frustrated me. After all, isn't loving others what we're supposed to do?

The notoriety arising from the article led to my being invited to Washington for a breakfast discussion of AIDS with President Clinton and Vice President Gore. I was the only evangelical among the sixteen religious leaders attending the meeting.

Given the fact that I had worked for Jerry Falwell and had helped write the platform for the Moral Majority, I knew that the visit with President Clinton would not be viewed with favor among my former associates, but this was part of my journey of love.

The person who took me upstairs to the breakfast told me that I would be seated next to the president. "He doesn't meet many evangelicals who are known for love," she said. "I'm so glad you're sitting next to him. Feel free to discuss what God is doing in your church." And I did. For the first fifteen minutes, while we ate, I talked to the president about biblical morality, Christian faith, and how to live it out in a pluralistic society. I told him about my journey, and he listened with focus.

While I do not feel at liberty to quote what he said, I found him to be compassionate and knowledgeable about biblical morality and its implications for American culture. The meeting lasted for over two hours, and God gave me courage to speak up for biblical morality as well as biblical compassion.

Our church was very supportive of my visit with the president, but when I was later quoted in *Christianity Today* saying some positive things about my perceptions of the president's spirituality, the letters began. It was as if meeting with President Clinton was worse than loving homosexuals.

A LETTER TO THE EDITOR

Shortly after my meeting with President Clinton, I decided to write an editorial essay for the *Grand Rapids Press*. It was entitled "Christian Church Should Show Caring, Compassion Toward AIDS Sufferers." After recounting our church's growing involvement in AIDS ministry, I noted how much opposition had come from other Christians. I concluded the editorial with the following:

> The problem with many Christians is that the issue of AIDS is an issue of "them" not "us." The issue of AIDS is an issue of "us." It is an issue of human suffering. What should the evangelical church do?
>
> First, we should *pray*. We should pray for those who are infected and affected. We should pray for those doing research that a cure would be found.
>
> Second, we should *repent* of our sinful attitudes and actions. We should repent of our silence and lack of action. We know that when we should do good and we do not do it, it is sin. Silence is sin. We should repent of our judgmental and condemnatory rhetoric and preaching.
>
> Third, we should *accept* those who are infected and affected. We should commit our resources and time to make a difference in this community. Your personal journey may be different than ours, but every church should be on the journey.
>
> At the end of a nearly two-hour meeting with the President, I had the opportunity of leading in prayer. I prayed for the President and the Vice President. I prayed that in the midst of politics and budgets they would see the face of human suffering. This is my prayer for Christians in Grand Rapids. In the midst of our plans, programs and preaching, may we see the face of human suffering and respond with love and compassion.[3]

Of course, my remarks only fueled further opposition. One person objected to my call for repentance:

Dobson's admonition that "we should repent of our judgmental and condemnatory rhetoric and preaching" is a clerical endorsement of the homosexual demand that we meekly submit to their distortion of reality and never say a word. We must agree with them that their behavior is nobody's business but their own, and that the consequences of their behavior are the business of the general public and of the public treasury. That is what everybody who reads Mr. Dobson's article will understand him to be saying, even in the event that he himself does not.[4]

I was shocked at the extent and depth of negative reaction and was not prepared for it. Nor was I prepared for the editorial that appeared in the local gay and lesbian newsletter. While the author did not claim to represent most of the gay community, I found his perspective, at least, encouraging:

Reverend Dobson at Calvary Church in Grand Rapids caused a bit of a controversy within the religious community recently by welcoming gays and lesbians to join in the services at Calvary Church.

This was not a move to accept the homosexual lifestyle as falling within Calvary Church's acceptable Christian behavior or even legitimize it.

Welcoming all to share in the Christian faith was a true act of Christianity and follows the Bible's teachings concerning the judgment of others. While the ideal policy would be to accept monogamous homosexual relationships and even provide for a joining of the couple comparable to that of a marriage, the move of not discriminating against people based on their sexual gender orientation is a giant step, especially for the hate-based bigotry which is so prevalent within the West Michigan religious community.

It sends an important message to the Christian community that bigotry and discrimination are not part of God's plan. It also promotes the concept of hate the sin, not the sinner.

It's obvious that we gays, lesbians and bisexuals disagree with the idea that our lifestyle is a choice as Calvary and most churches believe and preach. However, the significance is that Calvary Church acknowledges that homosexuals are human beings with rights, can be Christians, not void from God's love and not freaks of nature.

This is an example of the compromise I often mention in the column. Calvary Church has a right to preach and believe that homosexuality is sin, but they do not have a right to discriminate against homosexuals. They have a right to promote heterosexuality, they do not have a right to promote hate or bigotry against homosexuals or any minority.

As a community we should acknowledge this positive step and commend Reverend Dobson. We should also acknowledge that we respect Calvary Church's belief that practicing gays, lesbians and bisexuals are practicing sin; in return they must acknowledge that our community does not share this belief."[5]

CARING CAN TAKE YOU DOWN A BUMPY ROAD

The road down which our church's journey of ministering to those affected by HIV/AIDS has taken us has been bumpy. Because of the hazards involved, I wouldn't recommend that every church get involved in reaching out to those who are HIV-positive. Any ministry must be initiated and carried out under the Holy Spirit's guidance. The lessons of our first six years of ministry serve as an illustration of what happens when a church decides to love people who are treated as outcasts by many in the community. Here are some of the things we have learned.

1. *Christians are often better at hating than at loving.* A dramatic scene was played out on the evening news: People from all over America had come to rally in front of a prominent church. Famous ministers and politicians spoke of reclaiming America,

and, of course, the radical gay agenda was addressed. (For the record, let me say that I am opposed to the radical gay agenda. But it does not represent the feelings of all gays any more than murdering abortion doctors represents the feelings of all Christians.) Several hundred gays had gathered to protest the rally, and across the street from the gays, the Nazis had gathered and were calling the gays ugly names. A reporter interviewed one of the gay activists, who said, "I have more respect for the Nazis than for the people in the church. Both groups hate us, but at least the Nazis are honest about their hate. These people inside hate us just as much, but they smile and act as if they don't."

While I disagree strongly with the gay political agenda, I think this woman was close to the truth—Christians often appear more hateful than loving. AIDS, homosexuality, and President Clinton's viewpoints all seem to stir intense hatred among some Christians. I have taken the brunt of an outpouring of hatred from others because I insist on loving people. If people hate me, a heterosexual minister, that much, I would sure hate to be gay. I cannot imagine the hatred they must experience in their daily lives—and much of it delivered in the name of God.

2. *Christians say the dumbest things*. Several years ago our church was working with two HIV-positive gay men who were living together. They both accepted Christ and decided not to live together. They became celibate. These men came to church every week and became involved in a discipleship group.

One Wednesday night an outside organization used our auditorium and brought in a nationally known Bible teacher to speak. One of the men was in this service. The teacher spoke from Romans 1 and proceeded to declare that AIDS was the judgment of God on the homosexual community, a widely accepted position among the Christian community, but one I find to be both erroneous and arrogant. The Bible does warn about the consequences of sinful choices, but nowhere does it say that AIDS is the judgment of God.

The man we were working with was shocked and devastated. He got up and walked out. He continued to come back to church for a while but now has gone back to his previous lifestyle.

3. *The response to love is unpredictable.* Remember Ed, the former drug addict who met with our church board and helped launch our ministry to HIV people? I recall the Saturday night at church when I dedicated his baby to the Lord. It was the most unusual dedication I ever did. His wife was in a drug rehab program in another part of the state. Ed had HIV, so he knew his days were limited. And their son had an uncertain future. It was a moving moment. After the prayer of dedication, the people applauded.

As I write this chapter, Ed is still alive. His wife still struggles with drugs. And their son is growing up. Ed is serving a fifty-day jail sentence for failing to pay several hundred dollars in parking fees. Life for him has been a roller coaster ride.

4. *Sometimes the only people who appreciate love are the ones who receive it.* HIV/AIDS is a terrible disease. For many families with an infected member it is a lonely journey because they keep their struggle a secret. Bill was a very successful businessman who had lived a secret life of homosexuality. On the outside, he was a husband, father, church member, and businessman, but he lived with the nightmare of his secret life. Eventually he got AIDS.

His family responded with love, forgiveness, and understanding. They closed ranks, and apart from me very few people knew their secret. I spent hours with Bill. He poured out his heart to me and told me the details of his painful journey. I was with him the night he died in the hospice ward of a local hospital. His body was a shadow of what it had been. He occasionally opened his eyes, but I do not know if he knew me. I spent a long time with him and read aloud every passage from the Bible I could think of that talked about heaven. Then I prayed with him. I held his hand and said, "Bill, I love you, and I'll see you in heaven."

Although I appreciated the opportunity to visit at the White House, real ministry does not occur in the public arena; it occurs in dimly lit hospital rooms beside lonely people who are going over to the other side. And sometimes they are the *only* ones who know and appreciate your love.

5. *Love can make a difference.* Cheryl, a woman who lives in upper Wisconsin, struggled for years with gender identity. When she told her parents, they rejected her. When she told her pastor, he too walked away. She decided that her only option was suicide. One day she opened *Christianity Today* and saw the article "Ed Dobson Loves Homosexuals."

After work, she decided to drive to Grand Rapids. She checked into a motel with plans to commit suicide. But she wanted to talk to me before she died. *Maybe he can help because he loves homosexuals,* she reasoned. In the providence of God I was in town, and I met Cheryl at church. I connected her to another woman in our church who I knew would help her. Cheryl is still living and walking with God today. She writes to me from time to time. Whenever I get discouraged by the criticism, I think of Cheryl and many others who have found the Lord.

♦

Chapter 8

LET YOUR YES BE YES: THE SIMPLICITY OF TRUTH-TELLING

♦

Several years ago, Doug Fagerstrom, minister of adult ministries at our church, asked me to critique one of his recent sermons. He gave me the audiotape, and I agreed to listen to it and get back with him. I put the tape in my truck and ignored it for a while. Then I noticed that I had a lunch appointment soon with Doug. I decided that I had better listen to the tape, so I put it in the cassette deck and listened to the first ten minutes or so.

On our way back from lunch, Doug asked the question I was anticipating. "Have you listened to the tape?" "Yes, I have," I replied. I then proceeded to pontificate as I gave a detailed analysis of the sermon—based on only ten minutes of listening. Now I really had not lied—I did listen to part of the tape.

That same evening I was scheduled to meet several of our elders at the hospital to anoint a sick person with oil. One of the requirements in doing this is the personal confession of all known sin. The first sin that came to my mind was the deception I had used with Doug earlier in the day. I immediately asked God to forgive me, and I called Doug and told him that I had lied to him and asked him to forgive me as well. Whenever I think of this story, I get angry because I was so quick to lie in order to protect myself.

IS THERE AN HONEST PERSON IN THE HOUSE?

Honesty and truth telling are rare commodities in the world in which we live. Centuries ago Pilate asked the penetrating question "What is truth?"

Jesus was brought to trial before Pilate, and Pilate asked Jesus if he was a king. Jesus responded by asking Pilate if his question was his own idea or someone else's. Pilate then replied, "Am I a Jew? It was your people and your chief priests who handed you over to me. What is it you have done?" Christ then reminded Pilate that Christ's kingdom is not of this world. Pilate exclaimed, "You are a king, then!" to which Jesus answered that he was a king and that he had come into the world to "testify to the truth" (John 18:33–38). It was at this point that Pilate asked, "What is truth?"

From this moment on Pilate fought an inner battle. He knew the truth that Jesus was an innocent person and ought to be set free, but the crowd demanded Jesus' crucifixion. Finally Pilate gave in and ordered Jesus crucified. Pilate knew the truth (he was even warned by his wife) but refused to act on it. He ignored the truth for political expediency and personal ambition. He was afraid of the crowd and afraid of Caesar. If the crowd rioted, he would look bad and might possibly lose his job. Therefore he ordered Christ to be crucified.

Pilate's handling of truth is very much the way most people handle it today. Truth is ignored or distorted in the name of political/cultural expediency or personal ambition. Consider the advertising and business world. As I write this chapter I am sitting in a recuperation center in Almaty, Kazakhstan. The television is on, and I am watching commercials in Russian (I think). But the message is the same even if I don't know the language: If you want to look good, be successful, and have the right friends, buy our product. Consider the political world. Truth is hard to find in the rhetoric of most politicians. We assume that most politicians are lying until we can prove them guilty of the truth. In the judicial world the truth is often lost in legal technicalities, with each side posturing to influence the judge, jury, or public. And the religious world is not much better. Our exaggerations are dismissed because we are speaking "evangelistically." We use the truth to further our own agendas and personal ambition.

THE DEVIL MADE ME DO IT

We should not be surprised by the lack of truth in modern culture. In fact, there is a bit of Pilate in *all* of us. We are inclined to distort or deny the truth for the sake of personal ambition. Why are we so quick to carelessly handle the truth? We learned it from the father of lies—the devil. Jesus said to the Pharisees in John 8:44: "You belong to your father, the devil, and you want to carry out your father's desire. He was a murderer from the beginning, not holding to the truth, for there is no truth in him. When he lies, he speaks his native language, for he is a liar and the father of lies." When Satan lies he is speaking his native language. Since we were born into Satan's kingdom, we too learned this native language of lying. It is part of our fallen nature. When we met Christ, we were introduced to a new family who spoke the language of truth. But under pressure we sometimes resort to our first language.

I was fourteen when my family moved from Northern Ireland to the United States. I spoke with an Irish accent, since that was my native language. Over the years I have worked very hard to lose that accent, and today there isn't a trace of it left in me—that is, until I get tired and unconsciously lapse back into it. The same is true in our spiritual lives. In Christ we have learned a new language and a new accent, but sometimes when we get spiritually tired we resort to our original accent—the language of lies. Like my Irish accent, it lies beneath the surface of our lives and can emerge at a moment's notice.

We distort the truth in at least three ways: We lie to ourselves, to others, and to God. God values honesty in all our relationships.

We Lie to Ourselves

We lie to ourselves by assuming that we are part of God's family when, in fact, we are not or by judging ourselves more important than we are.

1. *Assuming we are part of God's family when, in fact, we are not.* This is without question the most dangerous form of self-deception, for it is to throw away our soul's destiny. Jesus warned the Jewish leaders of this religious self-deception.

> To the Jews who had believed him, Jesus said, "If you hold to my teaching, you are really my disciples. Then you will know the truth, and the truth will set you free."
>
> They answered him, "We are Abraham's descendants and have never been slaves of anyone. How can you say that we shall be set free?"
>
> Jesus replied, "I tell you the truth, everyone who sins is a slave to sin." (John 8:31–34)

The Jews were proud of their religious heritage. They had the law, the temple, and the promises. Based on their religious advantages, they believed themselves to be accepted by God. But Jesus reminded them and us that we all are "slaves to sin" and all need to be set free. While there certainly were advantages to being Jewish, the advantages did not guarantee a relationship with God. In fact, Jesus went on to say that Abraham was not their father—the devil was (John 8:44). Before we can be accepted by God, we must realize that we are sinners separated from God, and the only person who can set us free is Jesus Christ—the Truth.

This warning by Jesus has significant application to those of us who have grown up around the church. I often ask church people, "How did you come to know the Lord?" Some reply, "Well, I've always been a Christian." That is a theological impossibility. Salvation begins when you realize that you are a sinner and that you need the Savior—the only One who can set you free. You cannot rely on going to church, being a church member, or giving money to the church—these things are irrelevant to being saved.

If I were to arrive in heaven and be asked by the Lord, "Why should I let you in?" my response would have nothing to do with being a church member, a pastor, or a Bible student. None of my religious accomplishments would be of any advantage. I would respond, "When I was eleven years old, I invited Christ into my life as my personal Lord and Savior."

On Christ the solid rock I stand; all other ground is sinking sand.

2. *Judging ourselves more important than we are.* The second area in which we may deceive ourselves is in thinking that we are spiritually more important than we are. Paul warns about this in his letter to the Christians in Rome: "For by the grace given me I say to every one of you: Do not think of yourself more highly than you ought, but rather think of yourself with sober judgment, in accordance with the measure of faith God has given you" (Rom. 12:3). The key verb in this warning is the one translated "think of yourself." It means to judge yourself correctly or in accordance with truth. So Paul says, "Don't judge yourself beyond the truth. Rather, judge yourselves with sober judg-

ment"—or literally, "within the boundaries of truth." We lie to ourselves when our self-judgment exceeds the truth.

Paul's warning follows an encouragement to spiritual maturity. He told his readers to give their lives completely to God, to resist conformity to the world, and to continually renew their minds. These are necessary steps in our journey toward spiritual maturity. There is, however, an inherent danger in spiritual growth: assuming that we are better and more spiritual than the rest of the believers around us.

Some Christians assume they are better because they really are growing spiritually. They are excited about what is God is doing for them, and they do not understand why other Christians do not appear as excited. As a result they either develop an impatience with others or become self-righteous. Other Christians look down their legalist noses at Christians who do not share every detail of their list of external behaviors. Both types—"super" Christians and "legalists"—are self-deceived.

Paul gives the reason why we have no right to judge ourselves as important: "Just as each of us has one body with many members, and these members do not all have the same function, so in Christ we who are many form one body, and each member belongs to all the others" (Rom. 12:4–5). Everything we have, including our unique spiritual giftedness, comes from God. How can we be arrogant and self-righteous? Moreover, in the body we all need each other.

We Lie to Others

The second area in which we can be dishonest is our relationship with others. There are at least three ways we can lie to people.

1. *Blatant lies.* Blatant lies are what I would call "in your face" dishonesty. It is when you look someone straight in the face and lie to them. Peter did this when he denied the Lord.

Now Peter was sitting out in the courtyard, and a servant girl came to him. "You also were with Jesus of Galilee," she said.

But he denied it before them all. "I don't know what you're talking about," he said.

Then he went out to the gateway, where another girl saw him and said to the people there, "This fellow was with Jesus of Nazareth."

He denied it again, with an oath: "I don't know the man!"

After a little while, those standing there went up to Peter and said, "Surely you are one of them, for your accent gives you away."

Then he began to call down curses on himself and he swore to them, "I don't know the man!" (Matt. 26:69–74)

While the story of Peter's denial is familiar to most Christians, it is nevertheless a shocking reminder of how quickly we can lose our perspective and blatantly lie. The story is all the more incredible when we consider Peter's background. He was one of the twelve disciples, in fact, one of the "inner circle" (Peter, James, and John). He had been with Jesus for three years and had seen his miracles and heard his teaching. He walked on water with Jesus and witnessed the Transfiguration. He even declared that Jesus was the Son of God and said that he would never forsake him. Yet, when pressured, Peter denied Jesus and swore that he ever knew him.

Why did Peter fail so miserably? Because telling the truth had too high a price. He may have been afraid that if he identified with Christ it would cost him his life. After all, the antagonism of the crowds toward Jesus was intense. So to save his own neck, he denied the Lord he had followed for three years.

Before we come down too hard on Peter, we need to be honest with ourselves. Do we ever lie about our association with Jesus? Do we deny him when we are surrounded by people who may be hostile to our faith? On numerous occasions I have lunch with several businessmen who are not believers. From the moment I sit down until the food arrives I go through an inner struggle about whether or not I will pray before I eat. On the one hand, I do not want to offend the people I am with, yet on the other hand I feel that it is important to give thanks before I eat. Will I pray quietly and unnoticed, or will I pray out loud? Usually I speak up as follows: "Normally I pray and give thanks to God for the food before I eat. I would be happy to pray for all of us, or I will just bow my head and pray silently. Which would you prefer?" In almost every case, the people ask me to pray out loud. Even as I write about this struggle it upsets me that it is a struggle at all! But the truth is that we are constantly under pressure to distance ourselves from Jesus and deny our association with him. Such distancing and denial is *de facto* lying.

2. *Telling half-truths.* Most of us Christians do not regularly tell blatant lies. We are, however, often tempted to tell half-truths—not complete lies and not complete truth but something in between. We become experts at spinning the truth to serve our own agenda. Abraham, the father of faith, was an expert at telling half-truths.

> Now there was a famine in the land, and Abram went down to Egypt to live there for a while because the famine was severe. As he was about to enter Egypt, he said to his wife Sarai, "I know what a beautiful woman you are. When the Egyptians see you, they will say, 'This is his wife.' Then they will kill me but will let you live. Say you are my sister, so that I will be treated well for your sake and my life will be spared because of you." (Gen. 12:10–12)

Abram's strategy was quite ingenious. First, he did not tell an outright lie. Abram and Sarai had the same father but different mothers, so technically they were half-brother and half-sister. When Abram told Sarai to tell others that she was his sister, she would not be telling a blatant lie; it was true—well, half true; she was also his wife. Second, by claiming that Sarai was his sister, Abram showed his knowledge of Egyptian culture and law. If a man was a foreigner in Egypt and an Egyptian liked his wife and wanted her for himself, the law of Egypt permitted the Egyptian to kill the foreigner and take his wife. If, however, the Egyptian wanted a family member (one's sister or daughter), then he had to negotiate an acceptable price to get that person. Abram assumed that if he told the truth about Sarai, he would likely be killed. Thus he told her to say that she was his sister. If someone wanted her, he would set the price so high that no one would be able to take her away.

So Abram went down into Egypt with a foolproof plan. Well, not exactly—he had overlooked one variable. In Egypt there was one person who was exempt from the laws of negotiation— Pharaoh. If Pharaoh wanted a woman for his harem, he took her. No price. No negotiation. No argument. Genesis 12:15 records, "And when Pharaoh's officials saw her, they praised her to Pharaoh, and she was taken into his palace."

Now Abram was in a real bind. Pharaoh thought Sarai was Abram's sister, so he showered Abram with gifts. If Abram told the truth, Pharaoh would kill him. If Abram did not tell the truth, he would lose his wife forever. It was at this point that God intervened. Sarai was returned to Abram, and they left Egypt.

When we begin telling half-truths we dig a hole that gets bigger and bigger and bigger. Abram told half-truths to protect his own life. We often tell half-truths to protect our own character, which brings me back to the story of Doug and my dishonesty with him. It upsets me that I would so quickly tell a half-truth. After all, I'm a minister; I know better. But sometimes I have difficulty doing better.

3. *Slandering others.*

Now the serpent was more crafty than any of the wild animals the LORD God had made. He said to the woman,

"Did God really say, 'You must not eat from any tree in the garden'?"

The woman said to the serpent, "We may eat fruit from the trees in the garden, but God did say, 'You must not eat fruit from the tree that is in the middle of the garden, and you must not touch it, or you will die.'"

"You will not surely die," the serpent said to the woman. "For God knows that when you eat of it your eyes will be opened, and you will be like God, knowing good and evil." (Gen. 3:1–5)

We can be dishonest with others by lying to them, telling half-truths, or slandering their character. Slander is telling dishonest or distorted things about another person that destroys their character and integrity. Satan began his temptation of Eve by calling God's word into question. "Did God really say . . . ?" (Gen. 3:1). He then slandered God's character and good intent. He told Eve that God was withholding something from them, that if they ate of the tree they would become like God. He was accusing God of not being forthright with them and was thus undermining God's good intent. This is slander.

The Bible repeatedly warns against slander.

He who conceals his hatred has lying lips, and whoever spreads slander is a fool. (Prov. 10:18)

For I am afraid that when I come I may not find you as I want you to be, and you may not find me as you want me to be. I fear that there may be quarreling, jealousy, outbursts of anger, factions, slander, gossip, arrogance and disorder. (2 Cor. 12:20)

Get rid of all bitterness, rage and anger, brawling and slander, along with every form of malice. (Eph. 4:31)

Remind the people . . . to slander no one, to be peaceable and considerate, and to show true humility toward all men. (Titus 3:1–2)

Slandering another person, whether through gossip or labeling, whacks away at his or her character. Our culture seems to delight in elevating people to hero status and then cutting them back down to size—attacking them, slandering them, labeling them, undermining them, destroying their character.

We Lie to God

> Then Peter said, "Ananias, how is it that Satan has so filled your heart that you have lied to the Holy Spirit and have kept for yourself some of the money you received for the land? Didn't it belong to you before it was sold? And after it was sold, wasn't the money at your disposal? What made you think of doing such a thing? You have not lied to men but to God. (Acts 5:3–4)

We can lie to ourselves, to others, and to God. There is a substantive difference between lying to God and lying to ourselves and others. When we lie to ourselves we can fool ourselves. When we lie to others we can fool others. But when we lie to God we can *never* fool God. The story of Ananias and Sapphira is the story of two people who attempted to lie to the Holy Spirit.

The early church was generous in their care of needy people. From time to time people would sell pieces of property and give all the money to the apostles. The apostles, in turn, would distribute the money to those in need. One person who sold a field and gave the money to the church was a man named Joseph, a Levite from Cyprus (Acts 4:36–7). Ananias and Sapphira decided that they too would sell some property and give the money to the apostles. However, they held back part of the money for themselves and acted as if they were giving it all to the Lord. Peter describes this act of deception as lying to God. Let us note three things about this deception—the nature of it, the problem with it, and the results.

1. *The nature of Ananias and Sapphira's deceit.* Their dishonesty with God was hypocrisy, for they pretended to be more spiritual than they were. Their talk far exceeded their walk. Whenever we pretend to be more spiritual than we are, we are not only attempting to deceive others, we are attempting to deceive God. Jesus condemned this hypocrisy in the lives of religious leaders. He pointed out the main characteristics of hypocrites.

- They do not practice what they preach (Matt. 23:3).
- Everything they do is done for people to see (Matt. 23:5).
- On the outside they appear righteous, but on the inside they are full of hypocrisy and wickedness (Matt. 23:28).

In a sense we all are hypocrites. We often talk better than our walk. However, what Christ is condemning is the refusal to admit our hypocrisy and the determination to keep on living the lie.

2. *The problem of their deceit.* The hypocrisy and deceit of Ananias and Sapphira were rooted in two fundamental problems. First, they had given over their heart to the influence of Satan, the father of deceit (Acts 5:3). Second, they resisted the work of the Holy Spirit. Christ clearly identified the work of the Holy Spirit. He referred to the Holy Spirit as the "Spirit of truth" who would guide believers into all truth (John 16:13). Ananias and Sapphira had not only given Satan a foothold in their heart, they had also resisted and lied to the Spirit of truth. We do not need to give into the deceit of Satan. We do not have to live lives of hypocrisy. We have the Holy Spirit living within us, and when we yield completely to him, he guides us into all truth.

3. *The results of deceit.* You can fool some of the people some of the time, but you cannot fool God any of the time. God did two things in response to the deception of Ananias and Sapphira. First, he exposed the sin before the entire church. Second, he judged the sin before the entire church. The ultimate result was

that "great fear seized the whole church and all who heard about these events" (Acts 5:11).

What a powerful lesson on lying to God! God will expose hypocrisy among his people and will judge it severely. From Jesus' teaching in Matthew 23 and this case study of hypocrisy (Acts 5), several questions arise. If you answer yes to one or more of these questions, ask God to help you deal with your own hypocrisy.

- Do I talk as if I am more spiritual than my behavior shows?
- Do I do religious duties to impress others?
- Am I quick to judge people by outward appearance?
- Am I holding back from God what I know God wants me to give?

LET YOUR YES BE YES

Telling the truth to ourselves, others, and God all of the time may be difficult, but it is imperative. I have two formulas that help me to be honest.

1. *QLS²*. "My dear brothers, take note of this: Everyone should be quick to listen, slow to speak and slow to become angry" (James 1:19). QL stands for "quick to listen." This is not one of my passions. I frequently finish other people's sentences, which is a rude and arrogant thing to do. S² stands for "slow to speak." Again, I struggle with this.

2. *TKO*. TKO stands for "technical knockout." It is a boxing term that can also be used as a test for speaking. Before you TKO someone, ask the following questions in regard to what you are about to say: Is it the Truth? Is it Kind? Is it Obligatory? I have found these questions to be very helpful. If it is not true, do not say it. If it is true but not kind, do not say it. If it is true and kind but not helpful, do not say it.

THE TRUTH WILL SET YOU FREE

Jesus said, ". . . the truth will set you free" (John 8:32). Being dishonest complicates your life. Telling the truth sets you free. Recently I saw the movie *The Client* on my way back from an overseas trip. I am a fan of John Grisham and his work, so I was excited to watch this movie about a young boy who witnessed a Mafia murder. The Mafia threatens to kill him and his family, so he runs from the Mafia. The FBI wants to force the boy to testify, so he runs from the FBI. He hires a lawyer to defend and protect him, and she encourages him to tell the truth. In one scene he is put in jail for refusing to testify. His mind is overwhelmed. As he lays on his bunk he looks up and sees graffiti on the ceiling. In the midst of the graffiti are Jesus' words, "The truth shall set you free." He then decides to testify and tell the truth. He realizes that by remaining silent or lying he will be running for the rest of his life. Only by telling the truth can he be set free.

The same is true in our lives. Lying to ourselves, others, and God leads to a life on the run—from ourselves, others, and God. We live with the constant fear of being caught and found out. Telling the truth is what sets us free.

◆

Chapter 9

ENOUGH IS ENOUGH: THE TEMPTATION OF MATERIALISM

◆

I was sitting in my office before the evening service when "Fred" came in and handed me a gift. "I've been thinking about you," he said, "and I bought you a gift to show my appreciation for your ministry. Open it later." Fred was a relatively new believer. He is a physician and real estate investor. Like many new believers from unchurched backgrounds, he was zealous for the Lord.

The first time I met Fred was when he made an appointment to see me. He told me how he had come to the Lord and what God was doing in his life. He then asked me about the issue of giving to the Lord. "What are you supposed to do?" he asked. I then talked to him about the principles of love, grace, and generosity.

"That's okay," he said, "but exactly what should I give?"

"Well, a good place to start is by giving 10 percent of your gross income," I said.

There was silence. Then he spoke slowly. "That would be a hundred thousand. That's a lot of money!"

"It's not the size of what you give; it is the percentage that matters. It is no more difficult for you to give 10 percent than it is for a poor person to give 10 percent," I said.

"I never thought of it that way," he replied. "Do me a favor. Ask me on a regular basis if I'm giving 10 percent."

I had been in ministry a long time and had never had anyone make such a request. I agreed to do it, and over the next several months every time I saw Fred, I asked him about his giving. From time to time we would eat lunch together, and it was a joy to see him grow in the Lord.

After Fred left the office, I opened the gift. It was a Rolex watch—one of the most expensive watches you can buy. It cost about twenty-five hundred dollars. I was shocked. I sat looking at this beautiful watch. I had always admired Rolex watches. Now I had one. Or did I? I had recently preached a sermon entitled "Would Jesus Wear a Rolex?" Now I was faced with the same question.

I went to an elderly pastor for advice. He suggested that I keep the watch and engrave 1 Timothy 6:17 on the back. Concerning riches, this verse states that God "richly provides us with everything for our enjoyment." Then I met with three close friends from the church. All three are successful and wealthy businessmen. They advised me not to keep the watch. They felt that it would hinder my ministry. "When you're preaching," one said, "and people see a Rolex on your arm, what will they think? They'll probably wonder how you could afford it. They might wonder if you were interested only in money." "How about when you visit with poor people?" another said. "Can you explain to them why you're wearing a Rolex?"

After much thought, advice, and prayer, I decided to take the Rolex back to Fred. I was afraid of offending him since he was a new believer. I drove over to his office to meet him. "I've come to give back the Rolex," I said.

"Won't take it," he said. "I prayed and felt led to give you this watch. I want you to know every time you look at it that time is precious and a gift you give to God and others."

"But I can't wear it," I said. "It would be inappropriate." I went on to explain the reasons why.

"I don't care," he said. "When I give a gift I don't take it back. If you're so concerned about materialism, I'll drive with you to the Grand River, and you can throw the watch in the river. I don't care what you do. It's your watch."

The conversation went back and forth for nearly thirty minutes. It was clear that Fred would not take back the watch, so I decided that I would take it back to the jewelers. I would get less expensive watches for my wife and for myself and give the rest of the money away. Fred was agreeable.

I was relieved to find a suitable option, but I was not prepared for the morning I returned the watch. As I drove to the jewelry store a great sadness came over me. I had become attached to the watch and really did not want to give it up. It had captivated my heart. Even though I knew I was doing the right thing, it was most difficult to do. To this day I sometimes wonder if I should have kept the watch.

Living a life of simplicity in the midst of material abundance and excess is difficult. The attraction of material things can be captivating, as I found out with the Rolex watch. Knowing how to live free from material addiction is not an easy task. Even the simplest question becomes complex. What kind of car should I drive? A Ford? A Chevrolet? A Lincoln? A BMW? A Mercedes? A Lexus? Should it be a new car or a used car? What kind of house should I live in? Should I even buy a house at all? Would it be better to rent? The list goes on and on. In facing these questions I feel very much like Philip Yancey, who wrote:

I feel pulled in opposite directions over the money issue. Sometimes I want to sell all that I own, join a Christian commune and live out my days in intentional poverty. At other times, I want to rid myself of guilt and enjoy the fruits of our nation's prosperity. Mostly, I wish I did not have to think about money at all. . . . It hangs over me, keeping me off balance, restless, uncomfortable, nervous.[1]

THE PROBLEM WITH MONEY

In living out your faith you cannot avoid the issue of money, nor can you avoid the subject when reading the Bible. There are twice as many verses in the Bible about money than there are about prayer and faith combined. Jesus said more about money than he did about both heaven and hell. Fifteen percent of the recorded words of Jesus in the Gospels deal with the issue of money.

People who want to get rich fall into temptation and a trap and into many foolish and harmful desires that plunge men into ruin and destruction. For the love of money is a root of all kinds of evil. Some people, eager for money, have wandered from the faith and pierced themselves with many griefs. (1 Tim. 6:9–10)

The problem with money begins in the heart with a wrong attitude. Paul uses three verbs to describe this attitude:

- "Want to get rich"—the verb means to desire, plan, and purpose, to be consumed with the one objective of getting rich
- "Love of money"—the word means to have affection for or to kiss something
- "Eager for money"—the verb means to long for, strive for, and reach out for something

Beware of making money the central focus of your passion, dreams, and objectives. In the end you will be disappointed. Paul identifies the six consequences of running after money:

- You open yourself up to temptation and sin.
- You enter a self-imposed prison (a trap).
- You do irrational and destructive things.
- You are drawn into ruin and destruction.
- You wander from the faith.
- You stab yourself with pain and sorrow.

The biblical warnings against the dangers of money and material goods can be summarized in two words: control and addicition.

1. *The danger of control.* "No one can serve two masters. Either he will hate the one and love the other, or he will be devoted to the one and despise the other. You cannot serve both God and Money" (Matt. 6:24). Here Jesus compares money to God. Each desires control of our lives. We must serve one or the other; we cannot serve both.

In the New Testament at least three different Greek verbs are used to convey the idea of service. The first is *diakone.* It means to wait on tables and carries the idea of voluntary service. The second is *latrevo.* It means to work for hire and refers to employment. The third, *dovleo,* means to serve as a slave and carries the idea of complete submission to a master. It is this third word that Jesus uses to describe what money (or God) desires in our life. We will either devote our lives to pursuing God's will or to making and spending money. One or the other will be the controlling force in our lives. When money dominates, God's will is eliminated, and when God dominates, the obsession with money is eliminated. Both God and money demand total allegiance.

2. *The danger of addiction.* "Jesus looked around and said to his disciples, 'How hard it is for the rich to enter the kingdom of God!'" (Mark 10:23). These words are some of the most devastating that Jesus ever uttered. They were spoken to a "rich young ruler" (see the parallel accounts in Matthew 19 and Luke 18) who

asked Jesus what he must "do" to inherit eternal life. Jesus responded by reminding this man of the commandments. The young man responded, "All these I have kept since I was a boy" (v. 20). Then Jesus told him to sell everything he had, give it to the poor, and follow him. The young man went away saddened by these words.

Jesus' disciples were amazed when Jesus told them that it was hard for the rich to enter the kingdom of God. He said, "Children, how hard it is to enter the kingdom of God! It is easier for a camel to go through the eye of a needle than for a rich man to enter the king-dom of God" (Mark 10:24–25). This phrase has precipitated a variety of interpretations. Some think that the "eye of the needle" refers to one of the gates of Jerusalem that is particularly small. For a camel to enter the gate the owner must unload the camel so that it can squeeze through the small opening. Others think that the camel refers to a rope, not an animal. I believe that we should take Jesus' statement at face value. He is saying that it is impossible for the rich to enter the kingdom if they are addicted to their riches. But with God, the impossible becomes possible. "Jesus looked at them and said, 'With man this is impossible, but not with God; all things are possible with God'" (v. 27).

Addiction to and dependence upon money can be the major obstacle in following Jesus Christ. Several years ago I was speaking at the Moody Pastors' Conference. One of the evening speakers was W. A. Criswell. He spoke from this passage dealing with selling all one's possessions. At the end of a wonderful exposition, he con-cluded with some personal observations. He said he had been reflecting on the demand of Jesus to sell everything. He then told how God had blessed him and his family. They had a beautiful home. The church had given him a Mercedes. He had a beautiful office decorated with original masterpieces. He had box seats at the Dallas Cowboy football games. Then he pondered Jesus' question. "Would I sell *all* of this and give it to the poor?" he asked. After a long pause he said, "I don't know. I'm not sure!" I will never forget Dr. Criswell's brutal honesty. I feel very much the same way.

IS THERE A CHRISTIAN LIFESTYLE?

At times a vow of poverty is appealing because it would be an absolute choice and would make all other money decisions easier. But for most of us a vow of poverty is impossible. So we struggle continually to find balance in our possession and use of money and material things. When it comes to our lifestyle, we have three choices. We can live above our means, at our means, or beneath our means. And the Bible speaks to each of these choices.

1. *Living above your means is slavery.* Credit cards are in some ways the curse of the modern world! I get a regular flow of letters from banks informing me that I qualify for "their" card. Some even send the cards without my asking. It is this easy credit, along with slick advertising, that propels people into living above their means. It promotes a "buy now and pay later" mentality. For many families it results in expenses exceeding income and the gradual—or not-so-gradual—descent into debt.

While the Bible does not prohibit debt, it has no positive references to debt—only warnings. The most compelling warning is that when one goes into debt he or she becomes a slave to creditors.

> The rich rule over the poor, and the borrower is servant to the lender. (Prov. 22:7)
> The alien who lives among you will rise above you higher and higher, but you will sink lower and lower. He will lend to you, but you will not lend to him. He will be the head, but you will be the tail. (Deut. 28:43–44)

There is no freedom in debt. And when you make extravagant changes in your spending and living, there is no end to debt. The end of the month is a nightmare as you juggle the bills and realize you have more to pay than you have money. Randy Alcorn, in his book *Money, Possessions and Eternity,* lists the characteristics of debt.

1. Debt lingers.
2. Debt causes worry and stress.
3. Debt causes denial of reality.
4. Debt is dishonesty.
5. Debt is addictive.
6. Debt is presumptuous.
7. Debt deprives God of an opportunity to meet our need.[2]

The Bible calls us to get out of debt as quickly as possible.

> *Allow no sleep to your eyes,*
> *no slumber to your eyelids.*
> *Free yourself, like a gazelle from the hand of the hunter,*
> *like a bird from the snare of the fowler.*
>
> (*Prov. 6:4–5*)

The problem with debt is that it is rooted in greed—the desire to have everything we want now regardless of the long-term effects. Greed for larger homes, new cars and boats, designer clothes and watches, toys, vacations, fancy food and drink. Greed. Greed. Greed. And greed is always listed with other sins like envy, murder, adultery, sexual immorality, lust, evil desires, every kind of impurity and deceit (see, e.g., Rom. 1:29; Eph. 5:3; Col. 3:5).

2. *Living at your means is selfish.* Living within your means is certainly commendable and better than the slavery of debt. But to spend all of your money on yourself is an act of selfishness. The Bible repeatedly warns against self-absorption.

> What causes fights and quarrels among you? Don't they come from your desires that battle within you? You want something but don't get it. You kill and covet, but you cannot have

what you want. You quarrel and fight. You do not have, because you do not ask God. When you ask, you do not receive, because you ask with wrong motives, that you may spend what you get on your pleasures. (James 4:1–3)

Now listen, you rich people, weep and wail because of the misery that is coming upon you. Your wealth has rotted, and moths have eaten your clothes. Your gold and silver are corroded. Their corrosion will testify against you and eat your flesh like fire. You have hoarded wealth in the last days. (James 5:1–3)

Jesus taught that using material resources exclusively for ourselves is both greedy and foolish. "Watch out! Be on your guard against all kinds of greed; a man's life does not consist in the abundance of his possessions" (Luke 12:15). The word *greed* comes from the verb that means "to have more than necessary, to be present in abundance." Jesus tells us to defend ourselves against the temptation to accumulate more than necessary. Why? Because life does not consist in the "abundance" of possessions.

Then Jesus relates a story to illustrate his point (Luke 12:16–21). He tells of a rich farmer who produced a bumper crop and had no place to store the excess. So the farmer tore down his barns and built bigger ones. He then decided to take life easy. But God intervened and called him a fool and said, "This very night your life will be demanded from you. Then who will get what you have prepared for yourself?"

We can commend this farmer for at least four things: he wasn't living in debt, he earned his money honestly (farming), he worked hard, and he asked the right question, "What shall I do?" But his answer to this question was fundamentally flawed—it was selfish. Note the use of the first person in his language (*I, me, my*). "This is what *I'll* do. *I* will tear down *my* barns and build bigger ones, and there *I* will store all *my* grain and *my* goods. And *I'll* say to *myself*, 'You have plenty of good things

laid up for many years. Take life easy; eat, drink and be merry'"
(Luke 12:18–19, author's emphasis).

Living within your means and spending all your money on
yourself is not a Christian option. It is a selfish and foolish
lifestyle. It ignores others, eternity, and God, and will ultimately
bring God's judgment on our life. "You have lived on earth in luxury and self-indulgence. You have fattened yourselves in the day
of slaughter" (James 5:5).

3. *Living beneath your means is stewardship.* Living beyond
your means is slavery. Living at your means is selfish. The biblical option is to live beneath your means, which demonstrates
appropriate stewardship of your financial resources. Living on
less than you make enables you to invest money in others and in
eternity. The Bible encourages us to be generous with our
resources by giving to the poor (Prov. 22:9), to the work of God
(1 Cor. 16:1–2), and to world missions (Rom. 10:14–15).

If you are to live beneath your means, you will have to carefully practice two important principles: *restraint,* which involves
living within established boundaries (a budget) and spending
money prayerfully, and *generosity,* which involves learning to give
money and things away.

Many people buy what they want, when they want, so they
will not want. But the truth is that much of what they buy they do
not want. The first step in learning to live beneath your means is
to establish a budget. This budget should include all your
expenses—from housing and clothing to food and recreation. You
must agree to live within this budget regardless of how much you
make. If the money is not available in a line item, then you do not
buy what you would like to buy. You only buy it when the money
is available. Some people think that a budget is confining, but I
have found it to be the opposite. It is liberating! It frees me from
being overly concerned about meeting my obligations. I know that
I can meet them because they are in my budget.

Spend Carefully

Over the years in my journey toward a simpler lifestyle, I have discovered some principles that have helped our family in the struggle with money and spending.

1. *Set boundaries for personal expenses.* Have you noticed that the more you make, the more you spend? Then the more you spend, the more you accumulate, and the more you accumulate the more you want to accumulate more. It is a never ending spiral of making, spending, and accumulating.

Our family has found it helpful to establish boundaries for our personal expenses. When we are out of money for clothes, we do not buy more. When we are out of money for eating out, we do not eat out. When we are out of money for recreation, we do not go to the movies. When we are out of money for Christmas, we do not charge it and pay later. We try to live within the restraints we have established. I like John Wesley's motto which is paraphrased as follows:

> *Make as much as you can.*
> *Save as much as you can.*
> *Give as much as you can.*

2. *Learn to say, "Enough is enough."* The motto of our society is more like "Enough is *not* enough." You must drive the right car, wear the right clothes, bathe with the right soap, use the right cologne, and feed your dog the right nutritionally balanced dog food. Marketing is based on making us dissatisfied with what we have and then suggesting what we need to make us happy. How do we resist this trap? By understanding the minimal level of satisfaction and by saying no to excess.

The Bible tells us at what level we are to be satisfied. "Godliness with contentment is great gain. For we brought nothing into the world, and we can take nothing out of it" (1 Tim. 6:6–7). If we have food to eat and clothing to wear, we are to be content.

We must say no to excess in style and clothing. "I also want women to dress modestly, with decency and propriety, not with braided hair or gold or pearls or expensive clothes" (1 Tim. 2:9). In the first century when Paul wrote this letter to Timothy, braided hair was a statement of luxury and wealth. Women would braid their hair and adorn it with expensive jeweled pins until it contained the equivalent of a fortune. Pearls and gold were extremely expensive. Jesus told the story of a man selling all he had to purchase a pearl. Christian women were not to wear expensive clothes but to dress modestly and with restraint. And these guidelines hold true for Christians in our day. We, too, are to avoid excess, luxury, and items that make visible statements of wealth.

We are to say no to abundance. Jesus said, "Watch out! Be on your guard against all kinds of greed; a man's life does not consist in the abundance of his possessions" (Luke 12:15). How many suits and dresses do you need? How many watches and pairs of shoes do you need? How many necklaces and bracelets do you need? How many guns and fishing rods? The truth is that most Christians have far more than we need of nearly everything.

3. *Reject the messages of our consumer-sick society.* Americans are the world's greatest consumers. Although we represent less than 6 percent of the world's population, we consume 33 percent of the world's energy. Our air conditioners use more energy than the entire population of China uses. One of the powerful messages of our consumerism is that significance in life comes from owning and using the "right" products. For Christians nothing could be further from the truth. Our significance and value come from being in Christ—not from things (Eph. 1:3). We are blessed with spiritual blessings "in Christ." We must reject messages that tell us that our significance is in things that will be out of style a year from now. My dad has an interesting way of rejecting these messages. Whenever a commercial comes on television, he hits the mute button. The image is there, but the sound is not.

Another way is to speak up and say, "Wrong, false, lies," when we see commercials. However we do it, do it we must.

4. *Practice giving things away*. I learned a great lesson when I returned the Rolex watch. I learned that possessing material things is like dancing with an octopus. It's fun to start the dance, but then it is impossible to free yourself. Material things begin to captivate and control you—they possess you rather than you possessing them, making it difficult to break free. This is why it is important to hold things loosely and give them away regularly. When I returned the Rolex the jeweler was shocked. He had never known anyone to return a Rolex. As a result he began attending church and started his journey back to God.

Years ago I had a favorite tie that I wore every day. It was the only one of its kind I had ever seen, and I paid a big price for it. It had a picture of joggers on it. One day I was meeting with a guest from out of town who repeatedly admired my tie. Having recently preached on the dangers of material things, I stood up at the end of our conversation, took off my tie, and gave it to him. It was a freeing and joyful moment! Jesus calls us to live like this. Jesus said, "Give to everyone who asks you, and if anyone takes what belongs to you, do not demand it back" (Luke 6:30).

5. *Pray over major purchases*. I am the worst person to send to the grocery store; I'll buy everything that strikes my fancy at the moment. Maybe it is a "male" thing, but I tend to be impulsive. I remember the night I impulsively bought a 1949 Studebaker pickup truck and drove it home. My wife was not terribly pleased—to say the least.

One way to avoid impulsive and excessive buying is by learning to pray over every purchase. Will prayer mess up your buying? Ask God several questions:

- Do I need this, God?
- Do you want me to get it?

- Is it a necessity?
- Do I need it now?
- Could I use this money more wisely?

6. *Enjoy material things*. This principle does not seem to be in keeping with the first five, but it is equally important. As we live lives of restraint, we do not need to become antimaterial. Things, including money, are to be enjoyed (Eccl. 5:19; 1 Tim. 6:17–19). In fact, there is a passage in the Old Testament that no preacher I know has ever talked about. "Use the silver to buy whatever you like: cattle, sheep, wine or other fermented drink, or anything you wish. Then you and your household shall eat there in the presence of the LORD your God and rejoice" (Deut. 14:26). The Lord allowed for a time of somewhat unrestrained fun. The entire family was to have a good time.

Give Generously

The first principle in learning to live beneath your means is to practice restraint by spending money carefully. The second principle is to practice giving money away generously. Work is God's ordained way of earning money (Prov. 12:11; 13:4; 14:23) and his cure for greed (Eph. 4:28). Greed is getting and holding. Giving is letting go. The Bible identifies at least three dimensions to giving.

1. *Systematic giving*. "Now about the collection for God's people: . . . On the first day of every week, each one of you should set aside a sum of money in keeping with his income, saving it up, so that when I come no collections will have to be made" (1 Cor. 16:1–2). This giving is for "each one of you" "every week" and is to be in proportion to what is earned. In the Old Testament the requirements for systematic giving were clearly outlined. People were to give 10 percent of their income to God and his work. Failure to give was in fact an act of stealing from God (Mal. 3:8–12).

The focus of giving in the New Testament shifts from the concepts of law and obligation to the concepts of grace and privilege. The largest single passage in the New Testament on the subject of giving is 2 Corinthians 8–9. The word *grace* (Gk. *charis*) occurs ten times in these chapters and is the central theme of Christian giving. Grace is the model for giving (8:9), the enablement of giving (8:1–4), the privilege of giving (8:4), and the very essence of our act of giving (8:6–7, 9).

So, how much should we give? If the law demanded 10 percent, then giving motivated by grace should exceed the minimum standard of giving. Ten percent (the tithe) is the beginning point for giving. We should move beyond that as we grow in the Lord.

2. *Spontaneous giving.* "What good is it, my brothers, if a man claims to have faith but has no deeds? Can such faith save him? Suppose a brother or sister is without clothes and daily food. If one of you says to him, 'Go, I wish you well; keep warm and well fed,' but does nothing about his physical needs, what good is it? In the same way, faith by itself, if it is not accompanied by action, is dead" (James 2:14–17). Giving ten percent is a good beginning point, but it is not the final objective of giving. We should be open to generously responding to the needs of others as God reveals those needs to us.

3. *Sacrificial giving.* The highest and most difficult kind of giving, the kind that begins to affect our lifestyle, is sacrificial giving. It may mean giving up some meals or a new car or the redecorating of a room in our house. It may mean giving up a vacation or a boat or a Christmas present. It is the kind of giving that was practiced by the Macedonian churches (2 Cor. 8:1–4).

Paul has a special word to those who have considerable wealth:

> Command those who are rich in this present world not
> to be arrogant nor to put their hope in wealth, which is so
> uncertain, but to put their hope in God, who richly provides

us with everything for our enjoyment. Command them to do good, to be rich in good deeds, and to be generous and willing to share. (1 Tim. 6:17–19)

Rich people are to be generous and willing to share. One way to practice this principle is through graduated giving. Start with a budget that includes regular giving. Then decide that you will give away a greater percentage of what you receive above your budget. Maybe you will decide that you will give away 20, 30, 75, or even 100 percent of everything you make above your budget.

LIVING A BIBLICAL LIFESTYLE

Can a biblical lifestyle be achieved? Yes, but with continual struggle. Here is a summary of what we have talked about:

Spend Carefully

- Set boundaries for personal expenses.
- Learn to say, "Enough is enough."
- Reject the messages of a consumer-sick society.
- Practice giving things away.
- Pray over major purchases.
- Enjoy material things.

Be careful in applying these principles of restraint. Do not turn them into tyrannical rules. Apply them as principles in your own journey, and don't worry about everyone else.

Give Generously

- Systematic giving
- Spontaneous giving
- Sacrificial giving

A FINAL WORD

Material simplicity is one of the most complicated areas of our daily lives. There are *no* rules that make our choices easy. The above principles must be applied in careful and prayerful ways, but even then the struggle is not over. We continually battle against addiction and slavery to material things. The journey requires constant vigilance and reassessment. Don't be discouraged. It is not ultimately important that you *arrive* at a truly simple lifestyle. It is important that you are at least *trying* to get there.

◆

Part 4

FINDING UPWARD SIMPLICITY

◆

♦

Chapter 10

SINCERE AND PURE DEVOTION TO CHRIST

♦

Life in the Garden of Eden was not overly complicated. There were no thorns or weeds, no sickness or disease, no hypocrisy or deceit. Adam and Eve lived openly before each other and before God. Theirs was a utopian existence in Paradise. Then Satan tempted Eve. Eve took the forbidden fruit and gave it to Adam, and ... life became complicated. Eve would have pain in bearing children. She and her husband would be in competition with each other. Adam would have to fight the forces of nature to make a living and to survive. And in the end they both would return to dust. They were driven from Paradise and separated from the God who created them.

Paul uses this illustration as a warning for every Christian. He says don't be deceived like Eve. Don't let Satan lead you "astray from your sincere and pure devotion to Christ" (2 Cor. 11:3). The King James Version translates this phrase "so your minds should be corrupted from the simplicity that is in Christ." Satan desires to confuse us by leading us away from the purity and sincerity of our devotion to Christ. How can we maintain the "simplicity that is in Christ"?

THE SIMPLICITY OF KNOWING CHRIST

"For it is by grace you have been saved, through faith—and this not from yourselves, it is the gift of God—not by works, so that no one can boast. For we are God's workmanship, created in Christ Jesus to do good works, which God prepared in advance for us to do" (Eph. 2:8–9).

There is a significant difference between having religion and having a relationship with Christ. The key word in religion is *do*. It is a present tense verb. Do. Do. Do. You need to be baptized. You need to join the church. You need to learn the catechism. You need to be confirmed. You need to take Communion. You need to.... And the list goes on. Religion is based on the idea that we must do things in order to win the favor of God and receive salvation.

Having a relationship with Christ is not based on the word *do;* it is based on the word *done.* Everything we need for salvation has already been done. We have been accepted by God "through the sacrifice of the body of Jesus Christ once for all" (Heb. 10:10). I do not have to work to earn the favor of God. I simply accept God's favor (grace) through faith in the completed work of Christ on the cross.

1. *The basis of salvation.* The New Testament is filled with theological terms related to salvation, for example, *justification, redemption, adoption, predestination, forgiveness, salvation,* and *righteousness.* It is easy to become overwhelmed with these terms and to lose sight of the basics of salvation (knowing Christ personally). So what are the basics? First, as human beings we were created in the image of God. We have value and dignity because we reflect the image of our Creator. One reason we exist is to enjoy an intimate and personal relationship with him.

Second, we are separated from our Creator because we are sinners by nature and by choice. That sin began with Adam and Eve. It drove them from the presence of God, and it has been passed down to every generation of human beings since. God is holy, and he requires holiness as the basis of our relationship with him. None of us are holy. We all are sinners (Rom. 3:23). In addition, the holiness of God requires the punishment of our sin—death (Rom 6:23), separation from God both now and in eternity. All this talk of sin and punishment is politically incorrect today. People who talk about such things are considered narrow-minded. But this is what the Bible says. In fact, our sin and God's response remind us that what we do as human beings matters to God.

"For Christ died for sins once for all, the righteous for the unrighteous, to bring you to God. He was put to death in the body but made alive by the Spirit, through whom also he went and preached to the spirits in prison" (1 Peter 3:18–19). The third basic element of salvation is that Jesus Christ came to deliver us from our sin and to restore us to our Creator. Jesus was crucified (shed his blood) and buried, and he rose again (1 Cor. 15) to pay the penalty of our sin. God placed upon Christ all the sin of the world, and when Jesus died he suffered hell on our behalf. He came as the Mediator who would restore us to God (1 Tim. 2:5).

The fourth element of salvation deals with our response to Christ. We must confess and repent of our sin (Acts 2:38), believe the basic elements of the gospel (Rom. 10:9–10), and yield our life to Christ (John 1:12). For me, this occurred when I was eleven years old. I knelt by my bed one night and prayed a prayer that went something like this: "Dear God, I confess that I am a sinner. Please forgive me. I believe that Jesus died and rose again for me. Come into my heart, Lord Jesus. I receive you as my Lord and Savior, and I want to follow you the rest of my life." That was my first step in a lifelong journey of following Christ.

2. *The assurance of salvation.* One of my closest friends in life and ministry is Tom Mahairas. Tom pastors a church in New York City located in the middle of a city-wide crack cocaine distribution center. Tom was converted in the mid-sixties. He was a classic hippie—long hair, drugs, rock and roll. Upon accepting

Christ his life radically changed *overnight*. For Tom, there has never been any doubt about what God did in his life.

My testimony is very different. In fact, I have sometimes been envious of people who have incredible testimonies of changed lives. Not that I ever wanted to live their pre-Christian lives, but I wanted to have the assurance that they have. When I accepted Christ at age eleven, nothing in my life changed radically. I went to church before I accepted Christ, and I continued to go to church. I read the Bible and prayed before I accepted Christ, and I continued to read the Bible and pray.

For many years I struggled with whether or not I was really saved. I repeated the sinner's prayer over and over just to make sure. I have since found out that my journey parallels that of many like myself who have grown up in the church. I have developed a simple diagram that has helped me. It is called the faith and feeling diagram. Some people, like Tom Mahairas, come to Christ, and their faith is so strong and their life so radically changed that they never have feelings of doubt. Their faith always overcomes their feelings.

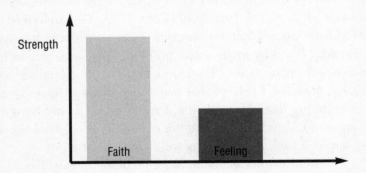

But then there are people like me. We accept Christ. We have faith. But often a sermon convicts us and we wonder if we are really saved. Did we pray the right prayer? Did we say the right words? Were we really sincere? Did we repent? And if we did do all the right things, why are we doubting? Our feelings continually overrule our faith.

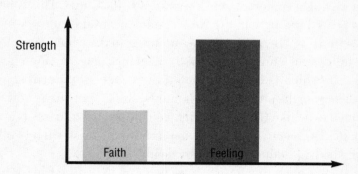

So what do we do? I discovered that the answer was in paying attention to my faith. I began reading the Bible and praying daily. This strengthened my faith, and my faith began to grow. The periods of doubt were further apart. Then one day (I do not know when) my faith grew beyond my doubt, and I never again doubted my salvation. If the devil can keep us in doubt and fear, he has distracted us from the simplicity that is in Christ. Over the years I have talked and prayed with dozens of believers who live in misery and doubt. They continually struggle with the assurance of their salvation.

WHAT IS THE CHRISTIAN LIFE ALL ABOUT?

Every business has a measurable, specific objective. McDonalds makes hamburgers. Ford makes cars. Dominos makes pizza. But what is God's objective for our lives? What product does God have in mind? Christlikeness. God's specific, measurable objective for our lives is for us to be like Christ. "For those God foreknew he also predestined to be conformed to the likeness of his Son, that he might be the firstborn among many brothers" (Rom. 8:29).

The word *predestined* means to "mark out with a boundary ahead of time." *Conformed* means to have "the same inner form." God has determined ahead of time that his objective for our lives is that we might conform to the likeness of Jesus Christ. This concept is repeated throughout the New Testament. God is at work in our lives until we "become mature, attaining to the whole measure of the fullness of Christ" (Eph. 4:13). Paul instructs us: "Put off your old self, which is being corrupted by its deceitful desires; to be made new in the attitude of your minds; and . . . put on the new self, created to be like God in true righteousness and holiness" (vv. 22–24). Paul's objective was that "now as always Christ will be exalted in my body, whether by life or by death" (Phil. 1:20).

God's objective for our lives is for us to be like Christ, to be godly; and part of the responsibility for attaining that objective is ours. "For physical training is of some value, but godliness has value for all things, holding promise for both the present life and the life to come" (1 Tim. 4:8). Paul tells us to train ourselves to be godly. He continues in this passage to remind Timothy of his personal responsibility to engage in a process that leads to godliness: "Set an example for the believers" (v. 12), "devote yourself" (v. 13), "do not neglect your gift" (v. 14), "be diligent" (v. 15), "watch your life and doctrine closely" and "persevere in them" (v. 16). This means that if we are not progressing in our journey toward godliness, it is not God's fault; it is ours. So how then do we train ourselves in godliness? Let me suggest the following steps.

Step 1: Confess and Forsake All Known Sin

Several years ago I decided to read from Romans to Jude in one sitting. I asked the Holy Spirit to impress upon me some of the larger themes of the Epistles. After finishing this endeavor I was strongly impressed with the New Testament emphasis on the importance of Christians avoiding sin.

In Colossians Paul devotes most of chapter 3 to the idea of "putting off " certain things and "putting on" certain things. We are to get rid of sin ("whatever belongs to [our] earthly nature," v. 5) and we are to put on the "new self " (v. 10). In Ephesians Paul tells us to "get rid of " certain things (4:31) and to be kind "and compassionate" (v. 32). He tells us to live a "life of love" (5:2), to avoid "even a hint" of sexual immorality (v. 3), and to live as "children of light" (v. 8). Peter writes that we are to get "rid" of sin (1 Peter 2:1) and "crave pure spiritual milk" (v. 2). John tells us that one of the evidences of our faith is to obey God and avoid sin (1 John 2:1–6). He tells us that if we claim to know Jesus, we must "walk as Jesus did" (v. 6).

Unconfessed sin is a major obstacle on the journey to godliness. It hinders our prayers (Ps. 66:18). It will rob us of our joy (Ps. 51:12). It brings the judgment of God (1 Cor. 11:30–32). In reading through the Epistles, I developed a partial list of the specific sins that are to be avoided.

Sexual immorality	Lying
Impurity	Stealing
Lust	Unwholesome talk
Evil desires	Bitterness
Greed	Brawling
Anger	Greed
Rage	Obscenity
Malice	Foolish talking
Slander	Coarse joking
Filthy language	Idolatry
Witchcraft	Discord
Jealousy	Fits of rage
Selfish ambition	Dissensions
Orgies	Hypocrisy

These sins have no place in believers' lives. They hinder our progress toward godliness, and they must be confessed and forsaken (Prov. 28:13; 1 John 1:9). Learn to keep a short account of sin! Whenever the Holy Spirit confronts you with your sin, *immediately* confess and forsake it.

Step 2: Discipline Your Body

Paul compares the Christian life to a running race. He tells us to run in such a way as to "get the prize" (1 Cor. 9:24). He then states that in order to get the prize, we need to go into "strict training" (v. 25). This explains Paul's final statement in the passage: "I beat my body and make it my slave so that after I have preached to others, I myself will not be disqualified for the prize" (1 Cor. 9:27). Consider the following translations of this statement.

> Like an athlete I punish my body, treating it roughly, training it to do what it should, not what it wants to do. (TLB)
> Like a boxer, I buffet my body—handle it roughly, discipline it by hardships—and subdue it. (AMPLIFIED)

Being a runner (maybe just a jogger), I relate well to this passage. From a runner's perspective, their are four categories of people in the world.

Spectators—people who line the roads during a race. They cheer and admire, but they do not run.

Joggers—recreational runners. They are involved, but they are not true runners or racers. At least they are more involved than spectators.

Runners—people who take running seriously. They train and know about such things as resting heart rates, maximum heart rate, interval training, and a number of other important concepts related to running. Next to their job and family, running is a central factor in their life.

Athletes—elite runners who regularly win races. Running is their life and their job. Everything centers around their training and running.

What Paul is saying in this passage is that we are to run the Christian life as athletes—elite runners prepared to win the prize. God does not want us to be spectators or recreational joggers. He does not even want us to be merely serious runners. He wants us to be athletes who are totally committed to the race of godliness.

Paul not only calls us to a disciplined life, he also identifies what needs to be disciplined—namely, our body, or flesh. Peter warns us to "abstain from fleshly lusts, which war against the soul" (1 Peter 2:11 KJV). The world of the New Testament was not much different than the world today when it came to temptations of the flesh. The Greeks had a god named Dionysius who was the god of pleasure. They believed that there was a limit to spirituality as perceived through our senses. Therefore, it was necessary to break through this limitation in order to achieve a higher level of spirituality. They accomplished this in two ways. First, through alcohol. Drinking was a means of breaking through previous restraints. The second way was through religious prostitution. The temple had official prostitutes (male and female) who would help worshipers break down their sexual inhibitions and thereby attain a higher level of spirituality. Drugs and sex—the same temptations people face today.

We are surrounded by pleasures of the body—food, drugs, sex, entertainment, TV, movies, video games. All of these things call for our time and attention. Some of them are inherently sinful and some are not. But all of them demand our allegiance. So how do we discipline our bodies to resist these temptations and distractions from godly living? Through strict discipline!

1. *The discipline of abstinence.* "Dear friends, I urge you, as aliens and strangers in the world, to abstain from sinful desires, which war against your soul" (1 Peter 2:11). We are "strangers and aliens" on earth. We do not belong here. Therefore, don't get too attached to the things of this world. When it comes to sinful desires we are to practice abstinence.

One practical way to practice abstinence is in the area of fasting. While food and the desire for food are not inherently sinful, certainly overeating is. To practice discipline in this area has spiritual benefit for other areas of our life as well. Fasting was both practiced and encouraged by Jesus. It was also practiced by the early church (Acts 13:2; 14:23). It is associated with repentance, prayer, and seeking guidance from God.

Abstinence can also be applied to time spent watching television, playing video games, or doing a hobby. The Scriptures even commend sexual abstinence for a specific period of time so that a couple can devote time to prayer (1 Cor. 7:5). In a culture that emphasizes self-gratification and the excessive indulgence of the flesh, godliness is cultivated through the strict discipline of abstinence.

2. *The discipline of avoidance.* "Flee the evil desires of youth, and pursue righteousness, faith, love and peace, along with those who call on the Lord out of a pure heart" (2 Tim. 2:22). When I was running races on a regular basis, I avoided anything that would hinder my running performance—certain foods, people who had colds, activities that might injure me. Those of us in the race toward godliness should avoid *anything* that distracts us from the goal (Heb. 12:1). This would include such things as certain books and magazines, TV shows and movies, conversational topics—anything that would lead us into sin (1 Cor. 10:13).

3. *The discipline of action.* "Not many of you should presume to be teachers, my brothers, because you know that we who teach will be judged more strictly. We all stumble in many ways. If anyone is never at fault in what he says, he is a perfect man, able to keep his whole body in check" (James 3:1–2). There is a striking promise in this text. If we learn to control our tongue, we will be able to control our body, and we will be perfect. The discipline of our body must include the discipline of our tongue. In fact, the discipline of our tongue is one of the key factors in disciplining our entire body. The

damage created by an undisciplined tongue is immense. Our tongue is like a fire, and it "corrupts the whole person" (v. 6).

One of the practical ways of controlling our tongue and our body is by practicing the discipline of silence. I have found this to be a most difficult undertaking. One night at our monthly church board meeting, I decided ahead of time that I would be silent. I would speak only when I was asked a question or addressed personally. The first item on the agenda was opened for discussion. It was an item that affected me personally, and before I knew it I had jumped into the discussion in an effort to defend my interests. When I finished I was mad at myself. Only minutes into the board meeting I had violated my agreement to be silent. Over the years I have repeatedly attempted this discipline with varying degrees of success.

Step 3: Stick to the Basics

All this talk of strict discipline would naturally lead one to think about a list of rules and regulations—things not to do, things to avoid, things to practice. Beware. Rules tend to distract us from godliness and sometimes become a god in and of themselves. The early church struggled with the issue of Jewish traditions. Peter broke down this barrier by preaching to and baptizing the first Gentile converts. But later Peter resorted back to adding Jewish rules to faith in Christ. He began insisting on faith plus circumcision. Paul was forced to confront Peter about his legalism (Gal. 3).

This is not to say that there are no rules. But the Bible teaches that *all* the law and prophets are summarized in two rules. First, love God. Second, love your neighbor. If we are to grow in godliness, we must focus on these rules first. If we learn to obey these rules, everything else will fall in place. "It is for freedom that Christ has set us free. Stand firm, then, and do not let yourselves be burdened again by a yoke of slavery" (Gal. 5:1).

THE MARKS OF GODLINESS

I realize that there is a risk in identifying the steps in our journey toward godliness—that they could quickly be changed into rules. But the Scriptures do suggest certain steps and certain qualities of what it means to be godly. Godliness is not *what we do*. I am a pastor, but that does not mean I am godly. Godliness is not *where we are*. Missionaries who sacrifice the comforts of our culture and live in relative poverty are not necessarily more godly because of their geographic location. Godliness is not *what we have*. We may have graduate level education in Bible and religion, but that does not equate to godliness. Godliness is *who we are becoming*. It is the process that gradually transforms us into the image of Christ. We have identified certain actions that facilitate this process.

- A godly person is one who confesses and forsakes all known sin.
- A godly person is one who strictly disciplines his or her own body (flesh).
- A godly person is one who focuses on loving God and loving others.

There is probably much more that could be added to this list, but this is about all I can handle right now. If I could consistently carry out these three actions I would be pleased.

Chapter 11

COMMUNICATION: THE KEY TO LOVING GOD

◆

John Powell, in his book *Fully Human, Fully Alive*, gives a list of insights that have changed his life. One of these insights deals with human relationships. He says, "The success or failure of human relationships is determined mainly by success or failure at communication."[1] In one of his other books[2] he compares communication to the flow of blood in our bodies. He says that communication is to love what the blood is to the body. When the blood stops flowing the body begins to die, and when communication stops flowing love begins to die. Communication is the essential element for keeping love alive in human relationships, and what is true in human relationships is true of our relationship with God. Communication is the key element in our love for and relationship with God. When it stops, our love begins to die and our relationship begins to deteriorate.

Effective communication is a two-way street. We must both listen and talk. We must hear and be heard. The same is true when it comes to our relationship with God—we must hear God and be heard. We hear God through paying attention to what he has said in the Bible—through reading, studying, and meditating on Scripture. We are heard by God through prayer. The Word of God and prayer are the essential elements in developing our communication with God and cultivating our love for him.

GETTING STARTED

There is no substitute for spending personal time communicating with God. It is one of the most vital things a Christian can do. I believe that it is more important than attending church, serving, giving, or any other endeavor. Communicating with God through his Word and prayer is something that we ought to do every day (2 Cor. 4:16). We need to consider a number of important and practical issues when getting started on this journey.

1. *Choose a specific time each day.* Some Christians approach communication with God as something they will do when they get some time during the day. The problem is that you usually do not get the time, or you attempt to do it at night when you are exhausted. You need to identify a specific time every day when you will read and pray. Mark it in your daily planner. Some people are early morning people, and for them this is the best time. My wife does it this way. I am not an early morning person. I read and pray better later in the day. It does not matter *when* you do it—just do it the same time every day.

2. *Choose a specific length of time.* A word of caution: If you are just beginning to read and pray, do not overcommit yourself to a long period of time. Start with fifteen minutes a day and make it an enjoyable and meaningful time. As you grow and cultivate this habit, then from time to time add five minutes. If you start

with a long period of time (one hour or more), you will likely get discouraged and quit.

3. *Choose a specific place.* Jesus told his disciples, "Go into your room, close the door and pray to your Father, who is unseen" (Matt. 6:6). You need a quiet place where you can be alone and be uninterrupted in your conversation with God. Several years ago I visited John Wesley's home in London. One of the rooms is a prayer room. It has a chair, a small table, a candlestick, and a kneeling stool. John Wesley prayed in this room every morning and every night. The room has been called the "Powerhouse of Methodism." Wesley wrote about the room: "Here then I am, far from the busy ways of men. I sit down alone—only God is here." Find a room or place where you can be alone to sit down with God.

4. *Choose a specific plan.* Some people fail in their communion with God because they lack an organized and disciplined plan. You need a plan for reading the Bible. You need a plan for prayer. Later in this chapter we will discuss how to develop a plan for doing both.

THE VALUE OF SCRIPTURE

"For everything that was written in the past was written to teach us, so that through endurance and the encouragement of the Scriptures we might have hope" (Rom. 15:4). This verse dealing with the importance of the Scriptures is written in the larger context of dealing with diversity within the church. Paul is discussing the issue of Old Testament dietary laws (Rom. 14:1–2). For Jewish believers, these laws were critical. But Paul reminds them that the Old Testament is much more than a book of laws to be obeyed; it is a book that gives us hope (15:4). For Gentile believers, talk of dietary laws and observance of Jewish practice was rather foolish. Their tendency was to ignore the Old Testament altogether. So Paul reminds them that "everything" in the Old Testament has value for the believer. He identifies four advantages of paying attention to the Scripture.

1. *The value of education.* The Old Testament in its entirety was written "to teach us." The Pentateuch, the historical books, the wisdom literature, the Psalms, the major and minor prophets contain valuable and important instruction. All of it comes from God and is "useful for teaching" (2 Tim. 3:16). The outcome of this instruction is that we will be "thoroughly equipped for every good work" (v. 17).

2. *The value of endurance.* Paul states that the teaching and instruction we discover in the Scriptures will lead to "endurance" (Rom. 15:4). *Endurance* means to "remain under adversity." The ultimate example of endurance is found in Jesus Christ. He "endured such opposition from sinful men," and he is our example "so that [we] will not grow weary and lose heart" (Heb. 12:3). Sometimes God will deliver us from difficulty and sometimes he will not. When he does not deliver, he extends an endurance that is rooted in the stories and promises of the Bible.

3. *The value of encouragement.* The Scriptures not only provide endurance, they also provide encouragement (Rom. 15:4). This is the Greek word *parakaleo*. It means "to call someone alongside," and it is the verb from which the word *paraklete,* meaning "comforter" comes. The Holy Spirit is referred to in Scripture as our Comforter. He comes alongside us so that we realize that we are not alone (John 14:15–17, 25–26). What is true of the Holy Spirit is also true of the Scriptures. They encourage and comfort us. As we read and apply the Scriptures we realize that we are not alone.

4. *The value of hope.* The teaching, endurance, and encouragement of the Scriptures all lead to the reality of hope (Rom. 15:4). When we speak of hope there is often a level of uncertainty in what we say. "I hope to pass the final exam in biology," a student says. "I hope to see you tomorrow." "I hope everything works out." "I hope you'll feel better tomorrow." Things may work out,

or they may not. This kind of hope is subject to circumstances. But the hope mentioned in the Bible is not subjective, and it does not have an element of uncertainty. It is objective and sure!

The New Testament identifies various kinds of hope. First, there is the hope that accompanies salvation, a hope rooted in Christ (Eph. 1:12) and held out in the gospel. Second, there is the hope of Christ's coming, the "blessed hope" (Titus 2:13) that offers comfort and encouragement in the face of sorrow and death (1 Thess. 4:13). Third, there is the hope of heaven, the hope of eternal life (Titus 1:2), which is the result of our relationship with Christ (Col. 1:27).

The Word of God is vital in our journey toward spiritual maturity. It is an anchor that serves us in the storms of life. It is a solid foundation for the building of our lives. It instructs us, gives us endurance, encourages us, and increases our hope in the face of despair. This is the reason Paul states that all Scripture is "useful" (2 Tim. 3:16).

Psalm 119 is not only the longest chapter in the Bible, it is also the largest passage dealing with the importance of God's Word. It identifies the four values of Scripture: teaching, endurance, encouragement, and hope. Read and reread these verses.

Education (Teaching)

> *I will praise you with an upright heart*
> *   as I learn your righteous laws.*
> *I will obey your decrees;*
> *   do not utterly forsake me.*
>
> > *(Ps. 119:7–8)*

Endurance

> *Preserve my life according to your love,*
> *   and I will obey the statutes of your mouth.*
> > *(Ps. 119:88)*

> *I will never forget your precepts,*
> > *for by them you have preserved my life.*
> > > > (Ps. 119:93)

> *Look upon my suffering and deliver me,*
> > *for I have not forgotten your law.*
> *Defend my cause and redeem me;*
> > *preserve my life according to your promise.*
> > > > (Ps. 119:153–54)

Encouragement

> *My comfort in my suffering is this:*
> > *Your promise preserves my life.*
> > > > (Ps. 119:50)

> *I remember your ancient laws, O LORD,*
> > *and I find comfort in them.*
> > > > (Ps. 119:52)

> *Trouble and distress have come upon me,*
> > *but your commands are my delight.*
> > > > (Ps. 119:143)

Hope

> *Remember your word to your servant,*
> > *for you have given me hope.*
> > > > (Ps. 119:49)

> *May those who fear you rejoice when they see me,*
> > *for I have put my hope in your word.*
> > > > (Ps. 119:74)

> *You are my refuge and my shield;*
> > *I have put my hope in your word.*
> > > > (Ps. 119:114)

GETTING A HANDLE ON STUDYING THE BIBLE

You learn to swim by getting in the water. While instruction is important, you will never learn to swim on instruction alone. The same is true with studying the Bible. While instruction and encouragement are good, you learn to study the Bible by jumping in. And when you decide to jump in, you need an organized system to help you get the maximum benefit out of study. Do not study the Bible in a haphazard way. Perhaps you have heard the story of the person who wanted some guidance from God so he decided to seek that guidance in the Scriptures. He held his Bible upright, closed his eyes, and let the Bible fall open in a random way. He looked down and read these words: "Judas went and hanged himself." This was not the guidance he needed, so he closed the Bible and let it fall open again. He looked down and read these words: "Go thou and do likewise." Distraught, he tried one more time and read the words, "What thou doest, do quickly!" While this story is fictional and extreme, it nevertheless illustrates the danger of random Bible reading.

There are a number of different systematic ways to study the Bible. Perhaps the most popular is to read through the Bible through in an entire year. This will require reading about four or five chapters from the Old Testament and two chapters from the New Testament each day. If you have never read through the Bible, I would encourage you to begin now. I have heard that Billy Graham reads five Psalms daily and one chapter from Proverbs daily. This means that he reads the book of Psalms and the book of Proverbs once a month. The book of Psalms contains human communication (prayers and praises), and the book of Proverbs contains divine wisdom. When you read them together you are studying human communication with God and God's communication with humans.

One of the most helpful study methods emphasizes studying the same passage of Scripture for several weeks. I began this method many years ago, and I started with the book of Philippians. On the first day of the month I read the entire book (four chapters). On day two I read the entire book again. I read it daily for the entire month. About day ten, two things happened. First, my Bible automatically opened to the book of Philippians. Second, I started to recognize what I was reading. I was amazed that on day thirty I was seeing new insights that I had not noticed during the last twenty-nine days. This method, reading and rereading, most closely resembles the concept of meditation. In fact, by day thirty, I had nearly memorized large sections of the book. After Philippians I went on to study all of the Epistles and the Gospels. I divided the larger books into smaller sections (four or five chapters). In all of my years of studying the Bible, I have found this method to be the most beneficial by far.

Having chosen a study plan, it is also important to develop steps that will actually assist you in your study. A simple structure that has been helpful to me is what I call the RAPP method of Bible study:

Read and reread.
Ask questions.
Personalize the truth.
Pray it.

1. *Read and reread.* I grew up in the Lord reading and memorizing the *King James Version*. I noticed when I read from the King James that I would often skip over verses or sections that I knew well or had memorized, so I decided to switch translations for my personal study. For a while I studied from the *New American Standard Version*. Then I switched to the *New International Version*. I also use paraphrases such as *The Living Bible* and the *Amplified Version*. Right now I am reading Eugene Peterson's translation called *The Message*. I recommend using a translation and a paraphrase or two different translations for study.

2. *Ask questions.* As you read and reread a passage of Scripture it is important to ask questions. Asking the right kind of questions will unlock the truth and enable you to apply that truth to your life. There are two categories of questions: preliminary questions that deal with the context of the passage and detailed questions that deal with the content of the passage. Preliminary questions would include the following. These are from the Navigators *2:7 Series: Course 4.*

1. What's the cultural setting?
   Does that cultural situation apply today?
2. What is the historical setting?
   Does it apply to a specific historical situation?
3. What is the context?
   Be sure you understand how the passage fits into the chapter and the book as a whole. Be careful not to apply Scripture out of context.
4. To whom is the author writing and why?
   Was it written to a group or individual? Was the author teaching, challenging, correcting, or warning?[3]

In answering some of these questions it would be helpful to have a study Bible and a Bible dictionary. A study Bible has footnotes, book overviews, and additional historical material. A Bible dictionary gives information about customs, places, names, and people in the Bible.

The second set of questions, of my own creation, deals with the content of the passage.

1. What is the main idea or point of the passage?
2. What does this passage tell me about God?
3. What does this passage tell me about myself?
4. Are there sins that I should avoid/confess?
5. Are there promises that are for me?
6. Are there warnings I should take to heart?

7. What are the key words and phrases?
8. What is the key verse?
9. In light of this passage, what is my next step in my journey toward godliness? What do I need to do?

I encourage you to write out the answers to these questions and then write a brief paraphrase of the main idea in your own words. As you study daily, you do not need to answer all of the questions every day.

3. *Personalize the truth.* Asking questions helps you understand and identify the truth of a passage. While this is important, you must also apply the truth to your life. James states, "Do not merely listen to the word, and so deceive yourselves. Do what it says" (James 1:22). The personalizing of Scripture grows out of the previous list of questions, especially questions 4, 5, 6, and 9.

4. *Pray the truth.* Until several years ago this idea of praying the Scriptures was a foreign concept to me. I learned it from my dad, who has been a pastor most of his adult life. He begins each day by spending at least two hours in prayer. I have seldom been able to match his devotion to prayer. Several years ago I asked him how he could pray for several hours. He then revealed his secret. "I just pray the Scriptures," he said. "What do you mean?" I asked. "I begin by reading, rereading, and meditating on the Scripture. Then I take the truth and the words of Scripture and turn it into prayers for myself and others. For example, if there is a promise, I claim it. Then I pray that promise in behalf of other people the Holy Spirit brings to my mind. I don't rush. I wait on God as I pray the Scriptures."

Eugene Peterson, in his book *Working the Angles*, has an entire chapter on praying Scripture. It is called "Praying by the Book." He says: "Prayer is not something we think up to get God's attention or enlist his favor. Prayer is answering speech. The first word is God's word. Prayer is a human word and is never the first word, never the primary word, never the initiating word and shaping word simply because *we* are never first, never primary."[4]

Peterson goes on to argue that we learn human language by being spoken to and we learn to pray by first of all listening to God's word in the Scriptures. He recommends praying the Psalms back to God. The last step in studying the Bible is praying the Bible back to God, into your own life, and into the lives of others.

THE VALUE OF PRAYER

When I was a student in college, a friend of mine invited me to attend the national conference of a major Baptist fellowship. More than two thousand pastors were in attendance and many of the largest Baptist churches in America were represented. It was a phenomenal experience—the singing, the special music, the preaching! I sat on the front row and drank it all in. One pastor began his sermon by asking, "Since this time yesterday, how many of you pastors have spent at least thirty minutes in prayer? If you have, please stand." I could feel the tension begin to grow. The auditorium grew strangely silent. I looked around, and no one was standing. Not one pastor had spent thirty minutes in prayer in the last twenty-four hours! Of course, neither had I. But then I was just a student—not a pastor.

In the twenty-five years that have passed since that service, I have struggled in the area of prayer. Several years ago I decided to devote the entire year to reading everything I could find on prayer and then attempting to practice what I learned. I read from every source possible—Catholics, Protestants, missionary pioneers, charismatics—anyone who had written on prayer. I learned and grew. At the end of the year I accumulated a mountain of insight but felt like I was still at the bottom of the mountain when it came to actually praying. I continue to struggle, but I have not given up.

A casual reading of the gospel of Luke and the book of Acts affirms the importance of prayer in the life of Jesus and the early church. Jesus prayed before his baptism (Luke 3:21), when the multitudes crowded him (5:16), before choosing the disciples (6:12), at Caesarea Philippi (9:18), at the Transfiguration (9:29), after the seventy-two disciples returned (10:20–21), as an example for the Twelve (11:1–4), and before Peter's denial (22:23–31). The early church followed Jesus' example by praying before Pentecost (Acts 1:14), after persecution (4:18–33), and when Peter was in prison (12:1–18). Both Jesus and the early church understood the value of prayer. Perhaps one of the reasons that we do not pray much is that we do not understand or believe in the benefits of prayer. What are these benefits?

1. *Access to God.* Job asks an important question about prayer, "What would we gain by praying to [God]?" (Job 21:15). What is interesting about this question is that Job essentially answers it by the word he chooses for prayer. It is the Hebrew word *paga,* and it means to meet with someone face-to-face or to have access to someone. The same word is used to describe the suffering of Christ in Isaiah's prophecy: "The LORD *has laid on him* the iniquity of us all" (53:6, author's emphasis). Here *paga* is translated "laid on him." It literally means that God caused our sin to meet Jesus face to face. So what do we gain by praying? We gain face-to-face access to God. That is reason enough to pray.

Throughout the Old Testament access to God was restricted. Moses saw a glimpse of God's glory on one occasion (Ex. 33:18–23). Once a year the high priest was allowed to enter the Holy of Holies to make atonement for the sins of the people. But through prayer and the merits of Christ's sacrifice, we have constant access into the presence of God. If God never answered a prayer or granted a request, prayer would still be a worthwhile activity. Just meeting with God has value in and of itself. We are encouraged to approach God "with confidence" (Heb. 4:16) and to "draw near to God with a sincere heart in full assurance of faith" (v. 22).

2. *Seeking the glory of God.* One of the primary reasons we pray is to seek the glory of God, not just to get things from God. I am afraid that much of our praying is focused on "getting." I call it Janis Joplin praying. Do you remember her famous song?

> *O Lord, won't you buy me a Mercedes Benz?*
> *My friends all drive Porsches;*
> *I must make amends.*

This is not to say that we are never to ask things from God. We are. But whatever we ask from God must be surrendered to the larger desire to glorify God. Jesus taught the disciples to pray with six specific requests (Matt. 6:9–13), and the first three deal exclusively with God's glory:

> *Hallowed be your name.*
> *Your kingdom come.*
> *Your will be done.*

The glory of God is the primary focus of Christ's high-priestly prayer. The prayer begins, "Father, the time has come. Glorify your Son, that your Son may glorify you" (John 17:1). Paul's prayer for the church at Philippi included requests for love, knowledge, insight, purity, and righteousness. But all of these request were for "the glory and praise of God" (Phil. 1:9–11). Prayer is valuable because it is a means by which we seek to glorify and honor God. The glory of God is more important than my personal needs or the needs of anyone else.

3. *Cooperation with the Holy Spirit.* True prayer is made to God in the name of Jesus and through the assistance of the Holy Spirit. The Holy Spirit guides our prayers by creating godly desires in our lives that will translate into our prayer requests (Rom. 8:5). The Holy Spirit prompts our prayers and brings us into intimate communication with God. We call God *Abba*—the modern equivalent of the *Daddy* (vv. 15–16). The Holy Spirit

interprets our prayers at times when words escape us and we don't know what to say (vv. 26–27). Prayer affords us the opportunity of cooperation with the Holy Spirit who indwells us.

4. *Personal transformation.* Prayer is a critical element in the process of becoming like God. Through prayer we are changed into the image of Christ. Oswald Chambers, in his book *If You Will Ask*, writes, "It is not so true that 'prayer changes things' as that prayer changes us, and then we change things."[5] He writes that a Christian is "one in whom the son of God has been revealed, and prayer deals with the nourishment of that life."[6] Paul had personal transformation in mind when he articulated his prayer requests for the Colossians (1:9–12).

THE ELEMENTS OF PRAYER

Prayer should be an integral part of our Christian life. First, we should practice daily time(s) of structured prayer. The Old Testament encourages prayer three times a day (Ps. 55:17; cf. Dan. 6:10). Second, we should practice intensive times of prayer that are devoted to a specific need. For example, Jesus spent the night in prayer before he chose his twelve disciples (Luke 6:12). Third, we should be in continual communion with God (1 Thess. 5:17). Each of these types of prayer has common elements that can be represented by the acronym RAPP:

Reflection
Adoration
Penitence
Petition

1. *Reflection.* We should begin our prayers by reflecting on the Scriptures. God always has the first word when it comes to prayer. Prayer then is my response to what God has already said (see "Pray the Truth" above, p. 158). In addition to the Scripture, I often use devotional resources as well. Some of the resources I

have found helpful are *My Utmost for His Highest*, *Our Daily Bread*, and *Streams in the Desert*.[7]

2. *Adoration.* The second element of prayer is the adoration of God. This can include two dimensions: *praising God,* which is adoring God for *who he is,* and *thanking God,* which is adoring God for *what he has done.*

The best examples of praise are found in the book of Psalms (especially Psalms 144–50). One can praise the Lord by simply reading these psalms out loud to God. Another way to praise God is by reflecting on his attributes and then responding with statements of praise that honor him for these attributes.

The staff of our church devotes a half morning a month to prayer. We spend the entire morning praying the Scriptures. About a year ago we were reflecting on the holiness of God. As we read and prayed several Scriptures, I was lead by the Spirit to the book of Revelation. I was struck by the words of Revelation 4:8:

> Each of the four living creatures had six wings and was covered with eyes all around, even under his wings. Day and night they never stop saying:
>
> "Holy, holy, holy
> is the Lord God Almighty,
> who was, and is, and is to come."

The creatures repeat these words over and over and over day and night without ceasing. I suggested that we follow their example. So for the next hour we went around the circle saying, "Holy, holy, holy is the Lord God Almighty, who was, and is, and is to come." We added nothing to these words and took nothing away. What happened was one of the most meaningful worship times any of us had ever experienced. We were caught up together in adoration and praise of our holy God.

We can also adore God by thanking him—for material provisions, spiritual blessings, our families, our health, answered prayer. The list goes on! Paul reminds us that we are not to live in a constant state of anxiety and worry. Rather we are to pray "with thanksgiving" (Phil. 4:6–7).

> *When upon life's billows you are tempest tossed,*
> *When you are discouraged, thinking all is lost,*
> *Count your many blessings—name them one by one,*
> *And it will surprise you what the Lord has done.*

3. *Penitence.* Penitence is the confessing of our sin, and it too is a vital part of prayer. Some Old Testament prayers were devoted entirely to confession (Ps. 51). Prayers of confession are heard and answered by God.

> To some who were confident of their own righteousness and looked down on everybody else, Jesus told this parable: "Two men went up to the temple to pray, one a Pharisee and the other a tax collector. The Pharisee stood up and prayed about himself: 'God, I thank you that I am not like other men—robbers, evildoers, adulterers—or even like this tax collector. I fast twice a week and give a tenth of all I get.'
>
> "But the tax collector stood at a distance. He would not even look up to heaven, but beat his breast and said, 'God, have mercy on me, a sinner.'
>
> "I tell you that this man, rather than the other, went home justified before God. For everyone who exalts himself will be humbled, and he who humbles himself will be exalted." (Luke 18:9–14)

Once upon a time two men went to Calvary Church to worship and pray. The first was a church leader and long-time member of the congregation. He parked his car in the shuttle parking lot and rode the shuttle bus to the front door of the church. Dressed in a dark pin-striped suit, white button-down-collar shirt, and a red striped tie, he warmly greeted his friends standing in the narthex. He found his usual seat, opened his *NIV Study Bible,* and prepared for the service. The choir and orchestra opened the service with an enthusiastic call to worship. He joined them in the singing of the opening hymn, number 295.

> *Naught have I gotten but what I received,*
> *Grace hath bestowed it since I have believed.*
> *Boasting excluded, pride I abase,*
> *I'm only a sinner saved by grace.*

It was a fine service! The man took notes on the sermon, marking his Bible. What a wonderful person he was! At the end of the sermon there was a moment of quiet meditation, and he prayed: "Dear Lord, I thank you for this great church. I'm thankful that we're not like other churches. We have a beautiful building, an excellent music program, and I sure am learning a lot from the Bible! I thank you that I'm honest, hard-working, and faithful to my wife. I'm glad I'm not like some of the other people I see coming here. I was embarrassed when I came in this morning and saw several people coming into the sanctuary in shorts. And that guy with the Bart Simpson T-shirt—what a disgrace! I'm glad I wasn't reared that way. I attend church on Wednesday and Sunday, I give my tithe to the Lord, I pray for the missionaries, I teach a Sunday school class. . . ."

That same Sunday another man came to worship and pray at Calvary Church. He was dressed in faded blue jeans and a Bart Simpson T-shirt. His hair was tied in a ponytail. He flicked his cigarette into the flower bed in front of the church and walked in the door. He was very nervous. Church was not his bag. He thought maybe he had made a mistake trying it. Everybody was *so* dressed up. But he knew he needed something in his life. He had been doing drugs for three years. His parents had divorced when he was ten. He had been thrown out of the house when he was sixteen, and the doctor had told him last week that he was HIV-positive. He was sick of his life and thought maybe religion might help. He had seen a billboard for "Saturday Night" and decided to give it a try. Now here he was on Sunday. The whole service was a bit strange. He didn't know when to stand or sit or what to do. At the end of the sermon, he quietly bowed his head and said, "God my life is all messed up, and I'm sick of it. Please help me and forgive me."

Two men left Calvary Church that morning. One talked to God and one did not.

4. *Petition.* The fourth dimension of prayer is petition. This includes making requests of God for yourself and for others. Jesus and Paul have given us some guidelines for biblical prayer requests. We are to pray for daily bread, forgiveness of our sins, and deliverance from evil (Matt. 6:11–13); for harvest laborers (Matt. 9:37–38); for increased faith (Luke 22:31–32); for unity (John 17); for deliverance from unbelievers (Rom. 15:30–33); for boldness in our witness (Eph. 6:18–20); for strengthening in the Holy Spirit, for a better understanding of God's love, and for the fullness of God (Eph. 3:14–21); for overflowing love, discernment, and righteousness (Phil. 1:9–11); for godliness (Col. 1:9–12); for power and for Christ to be glorified in us (2 Thess. 1:11–12); and for people to be saved (1 Tim. 2:1–3). We are also to give thanks for others (2 Tim. 1:3–4). These are specific prayers that can be prayed for ourselves and others.

SOME PRACTICAL ADVICE

Knowing the various elements of prayer is helpful, but what counts is putting them into practice. I recommend buying two blank notebooks—one for your personal journal, in which you can record insights from your study and reflection, and the other for your prayer book. The prayer book should be divided into four sections.

Section 1: Adoration. Devote several pages to the subject of adoration. In my prayer book I list different attributes of God for meditation each day.

Sunday	Love of God
Monday	Holiness of God
Tuesday	Mercy of God
Wednesday	Power of God
Thursday	Presence of God
Friday	Majesty of God
Saturday	Word of God

I also focus on a certain area of thanksgiving each day.

Sunday	Health
Monday	Salvation
Tuesday	Holy Spirit
Wednesday	Family
Thursday	Material things
Friday	Promises
Saturday	Jesus

In addition to the above, I often use a hymnal and sing hymns of praise to God (see Ps. 33:1–5).

Section 2: Penitence (confession). Several pages of your prayer book should be devoted to confession. My confession section has three areas of self-examination and confession. First, I examine my inner attitudes. I ask the Holy Spirit to convict me in the following areas: lust, envy, greed, gluttony, sloth, and pride. If I have failed in these areas in the last twenty-four hours, I ask God's forgiveness. The second area is in conversation and action. I review the last twenty-four hours and ask the Holy Spirit to reveal conversations or actions that have been displeasing to God, and then I confess. Third, I examine my yieldedness to God. I look at my emotions, intellect, will, imaginations, relationships, and work. I ask, "Have I lived a life that demonstrates that this area is completely yielded to God?" Confession is hard work, and it requires brutal honesty.

Section 3: Daily requests. The third section lists people for whom I pray *every* day. This list includes me, my family, and close friends. I write out my request and note the date. When God answers I circle the request. My requests look something like this:

3/17/94   I pray for _____ that you would give him wisdom in a job choice.

2/10/95   I pray that _____ would become a Christian.

10/12/95   Give courage to _____ to share her faith with her parents.

Section 4: Weekly requests. I pray for some people and organizations once a week. This allows variety in my daily prayers. My weekly schedule is as follows:

Sunday	Church services
Monday	Missionaries
Tuesday	Pastors/Christian workers
Wednesday	Government officials
Thursday	Christian colleges/seminaries
Friday	Friends
Saturday	Saturday Night service

Sometimes I devote most of my prayer time to reading the circled requests and thanking God for answered prayer. Please take these basic ideas, modify them for yourself, and start your own journey of prayer.

COMMUNICATION: THE WORD AND PRAYER

In the blur of daily activities and personal responsibilities prayer is often forgotten. In the early church, phenomenal numerical growth and social concern began to consume the church. The task of dealing with the needs of so many people overwhelmed the apostles, and they decided to delegate their responsibilities to others so that they could give their attention to "prayer and the ministry of the word" (Acts 6:4). Unfortunately the modern church and contemporary Christians are delegating prayer so we can give our attention to church growth and social concern. Let's get back to the basics!

◆

Chapter 12

KEEPING HOPE ALIVE

◆

Simplifying our lives is a daily struggle in which we must resist the natural flow of events that pushes us to run faster and faster. If we don't resist, the ever-increasing pace may cause us to burn out. Consider the factors we must face.

First, there is the general pace of life—hurry, hurry, hurry. I recently returned from a trip to Moscow. On my last night there I asked how early I needed to arrive at the airport. I was told that I should be there at least two hours before the flight. The reason? Because I would have to stand in line. No one was in a hurry there. I stood in six different lines—the customs line, the check-in line, the passport line, the security line, a line to go downstairs, and a line to get on the bus. The pace of American life is radically different.

Second, we must deal with the daily deluge of information. We are bombarded with the sights and sounds of modern technology: computers, telephones, faxes, TV, and radio. CNN reports the news as it happens, and we feel we must watch everything from court TV to disaster coverage. Our minds are saturated with information.

Third, we are highly mobile. Nearly everyone has at least one car. We are constantly on the run—to the mall, to the grocery store, to music lessons, to the movies, to school events, to church, or to our favorite restaurant.

Fourth, there is the breakdown of the family. We have lost a sense of community and belonging to each other. In Africa there is a funeral proverb that goes, "'Question: How many people does it take to rear a child?' 'Answer: The whole village.'" This proverb isn't true in America; our families are scattered all over the country. Many children grow up in single-parent homes. Families live in relative isolation and loneliness.

Fifth, we have the challenge of balancing all the roles we are required to perform. For me it includes husband, father, son, brother, pastor, runner, and Christian. Keeping it all in balance is at best a nightmare.

When you put all these factors together you have multiple layers of stress in your life. Is it any wonder that burnout is an increasing problem in our culture? Christiana Maslach, in her book *Burnout: The Cost of Caring,* defines burnout as "a cluster of symptoms, including emotional and physical exhaustion, depersonalization or a tendency to withdraw from people, and decreased personal and professional development."[1]

We all are vulnerable to burnout. About a year ago, as I woke up one morning and got ready for work, I felt discouraged—even depressed—but I could not think of a cause. I was reading the Bible and praying. Our family was doing well. The church was growing. I had no conflicts in interpersonal relationships. I was in good physical condition. I had no reason to feel down. But that is how I felt. And the feeling did not go away by the time I went to work. In fact, it stayed with me for almost a week. I even entertained thoughts of quitting my job. Then as quickly as the feelings came they went away. This short period scared me, and I turned to some close friends for help. I now believe that I was entering the early stages of burnout. What lifted me out? Strangely, it was a sermon by a guest speaker who talked about spiritual motivation. While much is written about dealing with the emotional and physical dimensions of burnout, little is written about dealing with the spiritual dimension of burnout. In the rest of this chapter I want to explore a passage of Scripture in which Paul talks about keeping hope alive in the face of pressure and despair (2 Cor. 4:7–18).

THE REALITY OF LIFE

> We are hard pressed on every side, but not crushed; perplexed, but not in despair; persecuted, but not abandoned; struck down, but not destroyed. (2 Cor. 4:8–9)

In these verses Paul uses a series of four comparisons to describe the difference between reality and despair in life's circumstances. Each comparison has two words. The first word describes *what is true* about life, and the second word describes *what should not be true.*

The first reality of life is that we will be "hard pressed." This word means to afflict, press, or burden the spirit. It describes the inner pressure. But we are not to be "crushed" by this pressure. This word means to press into a narrow space where there is no way out.

The second reality of life is that we will be "perplexed." This comes from the verb *aporeo. Poreo* means to go through. The prefix *a* negates the verb. *Aporeo* means "no way through." There will be times in our life when we cannot see the way through our pressure, but we are not to be in "despair." *Despair* is the same word as perplexed (*aporea*) but with an additional prefix (*ek*) that means "out of." *Ekaporea* means "no way through and no way out." While there are times when we cannot see our way through, we must never conclude that there is no way through and out.

The third reality is that we will be "persecuted." This word is a hunting term that means to chase down an animal. At times when people are out to get us, we feel like an animal being hunted, but we are not to feel "abandoned." This word means to desert someone under pressure.

The fourth reality is that we will be "struck down." This is an athletic term that means to throw an opponent down in wrestling or to throw someone down by force. There will be times when we will be thrown to the mat, but we should not be "destroyed." This word means "unable to get up." Even when we are knocked down by force, we should never lie on the mat. We can get up. Consider the following diagram:

WHAT IS TRUE	WHAT OUGHT NOT TO BE TRUE
Hard Pressed *(under pressure)*	Crushed *(no way out)*
Perplexed *(no way through)*	In Despair *(no way through and out)*
Persecuted *(chased down by others)*	Abandoned *(deserted under pressure)*
Struck Down *(thrown to the mat)*	Destroyed *(unable to get up)*
The Reality of Pressure	The Danger of Despair

The first column represents the reality of life. Pressure, problems, disappointments, and failures are inevitable. The second column represents a life of despair. We must avoid living in column two. My observation is that the pressures of life are continually pushing us from column one to column two. We are always in danger of giving in to despair. How do we avoid despair? By keeping hope alive. The missing ingredient in column two is hope. When we live in column two we have lost hope. If we maintain hope, we will resist the natural slide into despair. In 2 Corinthians 4:7–18 Paul identifies five biblical principles that will help keep hope alive.

Principle 1: Understand the Limitations of the Jar of Clay

> But we have this treasure in jars of clay to show that
> this all-surpassing power is from God and not from us.
> (2 Cor. 4:7)

The city of Corinth was known throughout the ancient world for its pottery factories. Their specialty was making small, fragile lamps. These were beautiful but easily broken. This is the imagery Paul uses to describe our physical bodies. The treasure (Christ) is in a "jar of clay"—a fragile and easily broken piece of pottery. The first principle for keeping hope alive is to understand that our physical bodies have limitations—they are fragile and easily broken.

First, we have physical limitations. We need a certain amount of sleep, balanced meals, physical exercise, and time off each week to rest and play. If we keep violating these basic physical limitations, the jar of clay will eventually break down.

Second, we have time limitations. We all have twenty-four hours per day. I have discovered that there is never enough time to do everything, but there is always enough time to do what is important. You cannot please everyone or be everywhere. You have to recognize your limitations and make the most important choices. I remember the first time our daughter had a school activity the same night I had a church board meeting. The board meeting started at 7:00 and Heather's event started at 7:30. I needed to be at both places, so I first went to the board meeting and explained my dilemma. I told the board that I needed to attend Heather's event and that after it was over I would come back to the board meeting. When I went back to the board meeting it was over! The board really didn't need me, but Heather did!

Principle 2: Focus on What God Is Doing *in* You, Not *Through* You

> We always carry around in our body the death of Jesus, so that the life of Jesus may also be revealed in our body. For we who are alive are always being given over to death for Jesus' sake, so that his life may be revealed in our mortal body. (2 Cor. 4:10–11)

What is spiritual success? In pastoral ministry success is often measured by external criteria. Is the church growing numerically? Are the offerings increasing? Is membership up? Are baptisms up over last year? All these questions focus on the outward. They reflect, in part, what God is doing *through* a person or church. But this is not God's priority. God is much more interested in what he is doing *in* us than in what he is doing *through* us. God's objective is that "the life of Jesus may also be revealed in our body" (2 Cor. 4:10).

The verb translated "revealed" is the Greek verb *phaneroo*. It means to make clear or bring into focus. God wants to bring the life of Jesus into closer focus in our bodies. He is in the process of making us like Jesus Christ (Rom. 8:28–30). When pressure builds and stress accumulates we can easily lose our focus. We can be so consumed by the outward that we forget about the inward. God is still at work in our lives to make the life of Jesus clear.

When Paul wrote the book of Philippians he was under pressure. He was in prison, and his future was uncertain. He was being criticized by other Christian believers who were bent on destroying his character and reputation. But Paul was not in despair. In fact, the theme of the book of Philippians is "joy." Paul understood that God was still at work in his life in spite of the fact that he was prevented from traveling and planting churches. Paul knew the priority of God's inward work and wrote, "I eagerly expect and hope that I will in no way be ashamed, but will have sufficient courage so that now as always Christ will be exalted in my body, whether by life or by death" (Phil. 1:20).

Jonah is an example of someone through whom God did a mighty work but who missed out on what God wanted to do in him. Although Jonah resisted the call of God, he eventually went to Nineveh to preach a message of impending judgment. Jonah predicted that within four days the city would be overthrown. God blessed Jonah's preaching, and the entire city believed and turned to God. The king made this proclamation: "But let man and beast be covered with sackcloth. Let everyone call urgently on God. Let them give up their evil ways and their violence. Who knows? God may yet relent and with compassion turn from his fierce anger so that we will not perish" (Jonah 3:8–9). Imagine—an entire pagan city turned to God through the preaching of a Jewish prophet. This was success!

You would think Jonah would be happy. But he wasn't. He was angry with God for sparing the city. In fact, he was angry enough to die (Jonah 4:9). Jonah resisted the work that God wanted to do in his life in spite of his outward success. He missed out on the heart and compassion of God—something God wanted to cultivate in the prophet's life (Jonah 4:10–11).

God does his inward work in good times and bad times. Whether we are outwardly successful or not, God is still at work in our lives. He wants to chip away at the corners of our life that do not reflect Jesus Christ. And he will keep chipping away until the fullness of Christ's life appears in our body.

Principle 3: Cultivate the Spirit of Faith

> It is written: "I believed; therefore I have spoken."
> With that same spirit of faith we also believe and therefore
> speak. . . ." (2 Cor. 4:13)

We can help keep hope alive by cultivating and maintaining a spirit of faith. This is much more than maintaining a positive attitude. While it is true that a positive mental attitude is helpful in the battle against despair, a spirit of faith is far more important. A spirit of faith is a spirit of confident trust in God and his promises.

In introducing this concept, Paul quotes from the book of Psalms. "I believed; therefore I said" (Ps. 116:10). The first part of the psalm describes the writer's dilemma. The writer was "overcome by trouble and sorrow" and "the cords of death entangled [him]" (116:3). He was facing despair and death. But in the face of such anguish, he called out to the Lord and then offered a fitting tribute to the Lord.

> *I will sacrifice a thank offering to you*
> *and call on the name of the LORD.*
> *I will fulfill my vows to the LORD*
> *in the presence of all his people,*
> *in the courts of the house of the LORD—*
> *in your midst, O Jerusalem.*
>
> *Praise the LORD.*
>
> *(Ps. 116:17–19)*

Between the despair and the offering of praise he said, "I believed." He believed in the faithfulness and mercy of God and therefore was able to speak of God's deliverance even before it occurred. This is the spirit of faith. Before God delivers, in the midst of despair, we can believe and declare God's faithfulness, knowing that God will not let us down.

How do you maintain and cultivate the spirit of faith in the face of despair? Paul identifies four elements that enhance the spirit of faith. "With that same spirit of faith we also believe and therefore speak, *because* we know that the one who raised the Lord Jesus from the dead will also raise us with Jesus and present us with you in his presence" (2 Cor. 4:13–14, author's emphasis).

The first element that enhances the spirit of faith is the resurrection of Jesus Christ. Christianity and Christian hope are not based on a series of abstract theological propositions. Rather, they are based on the historical reality of the resurrection of Jesus Christ. Our hope is anchored to this event.

The second element that enhances faith is our own resurrection, which is vitally connected to the resurrection of Christ. In facing the despair of life, the worst-case scenario is disease and death. But for the Christian, the worst is not the worst, the worst becomes the best. Death does not end it. Death is the pathway to the presence of God, which is "better by far" (Phil. 1:23).

The third element that enhances faith is the sustaining grace of God, a grace that is "reaching more and more people" (2 Cor. 4:15). For the believer, God's grace is his supernatural, undeserved favor and strength on our behalf. Sometimes God does not alter our circumstances, but he always extends grace to help us endure and to deliver us from despair. God did not answer Paul's prayer for deliverance from a "thorn in the flesh, " but he did give Paul a promise: "But he said to me, 'My grace is sufficient for you, for my power is made perfect in weakness.' Therefore I will boast all the more gladly about my weaknesses, so that Christ's power may rest on me. That is why, for Christ's sake, I delight in weaknesses, in insults, in hardships, in persecutions, in difficulties. For when I am weak, then I am strong" (2 Cor. 12:9–10).

The fourth element that enhances the spirit of faith is thanksgiving—a thanksgiving that overflows to "the glory of God" (2 Cor. 4:15). The spirit of faith can be increased and sustained in the most adverse of circumstances by giving thanks to God. Thanksgiving can change our attitude. We tend to be overcome with the negative, but we can overcome the negative by giving thanks to God for all the good things he has done.

I learned this lesson of thanksgiving early in my spiritual journey. One day I came home from work immensely discouraged by the events of the day. Every decision I had made was overturned without consulting me or asking for my input. It was as if my opinion was irrelevant. Moreover, I found out about the decisions from someone outside my department. I was angry and discouraged.

I went to my bedroom to read and pray, but I could not do it. The circumstances of the day consumed me. Then I read Philippians. The call to prayer impressed me. "Do not be anxious about anything, but in everything, by prayer and petition, with thanksgiving, present your requests to God. And the peace of God, which transcends all understanding, will guard your hearts and your minds in Christ Jesus" (4:6–7).

What struck me was the phrase "with thanksgiving." I decided to take the phrase literally. I began thanking God for all the material things in my bedroom—the bed, the box springs, the mattress, the sheets, the pillows, the pillow cases, the blanket, the bedspread, the carpet, the dresser, the contents of each dresser drawer, my socks, my underwear (each item individually). Then I went to my closet and thanked God for each individual suit, coat, pair of slacks, and shirt. I thanked God for *everything* in one room. In the process of this simple exercise, something supernatural happened. The despair faded into insignificance, and I was overwhelmed by the goodness of God. And this was just one room of our home. I did not get to the other rooms. I did not get to the spiritual blessings that are far more significant than the material ones.

Christians can face the greatest despair with a spirit of faith. Jesus is alive! We will be raised with him in the great resurrection! We are recipients of the overflowing grace of God! We have *much* for which to be thankful.

Principle 4: Live One Day at a Time

> Therefore we do not lose heart. Though outwardly we are wasting away, yet inwardly we are being renewed day by day. (2 Cor. 4:16)

The older I get the more I realize that my physical body is "wasting away." Last summer I played with my oldest son on an adult soccer team. I thoroughly enjoyed playing with my son, but I was a step slower than the rest. It also took several days to get over the soreness after each game. The bad news is that from now on my vitality will be going downhill. The good news is that I can still grow and be renewed inwardly—day by day.

There are no shortcuts to holiness, no giant steps that will bring balance to our frenzied lives. There are no simple answers for a simple lifestyle. There is only the opportunity to make little choices every day, to take one step at a time. The Christian life is not a one-hundred-yard sprint. It is a marathon. And a marathon is run one step at a time and one mile at a time. Do not expect instant success. Trust God for each day.

Principle 5: Fix Your Hope On Eternity

> For our light and momentary troubles are achieving for us an eternal glory that far outweighs them all. So we fix our eyes not on what is seen, but on what is unseen. For what is seen is temporary, but what is unseen is eternal. (2 Cor. 4:17–18)

When facing the despair of our current circumstances, we must remember that all trouble, however bad, is only temporary. Our destination is heaven, and when we get there the worst we endured down here will be outweighed by that glory. Trouble is not permanent. It too will pass. What matters is the eternal, because heaven will last forever and will be free of all trouble (Rev. 21:4–5).

The hope of eternity has been a vital ingredient in the lives of people of faith. It has sustained them and given them hope. It sustained Abram as he traveled the Promised Land as a stranger. He was "looking forward to the city with foundations, whose architect and builder is God" (Heb. 11:9–10). The same is true of many others listed in Hebrews 11. They had a forward, upward, and eternal look. They were "longing for a better country—a heavenly one" (v. 16).

CONCLUSION

The pressures of life left unchecked will push us into despair. In the face of that potential for despair, it is imperative that we keep hope alive. And we can. First, we must live with the limitations of our physical body. No one is a superperson. Jump off the building like Superman, and you will crash. Second, we must focus on God's inward work of making us more and more like Jesus Christ. Often the most significant steps in this process occur under stress. Third, we must cultivate the spirit of faith. Christians have every reason for faith and not doubt. Fourth, we can live only one day at a time. There are no shortcuts. Fifth, our future hope is eternity. This world is not our home. We are headed for heaven. So keep your head up, your glance forward, and your passion for heaven.

◆

What Now?

Simplicity is fundamentally a process of getting rid of the duplicity in our lives—both inward and outward. It is a conscious and deliberate refusal to chase the American dream of more and more and more. Charlotte Davis Kasl puts it in perspective.

> There was a cartoon in the *New Yorker* portraying a man running toward the end of the rainbow only to see a pot of baked beans there. Whenever I think of striving for something I think of that image and realize it's time to stop, breathe, and remember there's beauty in the ordinary.
>
> Recently I visited a dear old friend. His sense of graciousness and ritual was as I remembered. I had mentioned that I wanted only fruit tea for breakfast, and I arrived to a neatly set table with an orange and apple on a plate beside a knife, a mug, and a newspaper on the same green tablecloth I had sat at 25 years before. I also saw the same bookshelves, the same tables, the same dishes, and the same couch as before. In a passing moment, a painful image flashed through my mind of the thousand of dollars I had spent on such items over the years and how little they mattered. How peaceful it was to be with him in this uncluttered home. I hold that image as I struggle to detach from wanting more things.[1]

What is true of material things is also true of our relationship to God and others. We keep adding layers. In the journey toward more authentic living, I have discovered several principles.

1. *Simplicity is a process—not an event.* Having read volumes on the subject of simplicity and its implications for everyday life, I have yet to find a person who claimed to have fully achieved the objective of simplicity. Whenever I get discouraged, I remind myself that this is a journey—not a one-time event. The most important issue is whether or not I am on the journey.

2. *Simplicity requires vigilance.* The second law of thermodynamics states that things in life break down and become more disorderly—they do not get better. This holds true in the area of simplicity. Without effort and vigilance the state of duplicity continually increases. We must constantly make choices that resist duplicity.

3. *Simplicity is worth the effort.* Simplicity is freedom. Simplicity is joy. Simplicity is peace. And while it requires painful choices and outward vigilance, it is worth the effort. Charlotte Davis Kasl puts it this way:

> So next time you sit down to a simple supper, crawl into a cozy bed, have a warm chat with a friend—imagine that you *are* at the end of the rainbow. This is it. This is life, and it's wonderful just in this moment.[2]

◆

Notes

Chapter 1 I'm Running As Fast As I Can

[1]Urban T. Holmes III, *Spirituality for Ministry* (New York: Harper & Row, 1982), as quoted in Reuben P. Job and Norman Shawchuck, *A Guide to Prayer* (Nashville: Upper Room, 1983), 137.

[2]George Sheehan, *Getting Fit and Feeling Good* (New York: Wings Books, 1992), 31.

[3]Albert E. Day, *Discipline and Discovery* (Nashville: Upper Room, 1977), as quoted in Job and Shawchuck, *A Guide to Prayer.*

[4]Richard Foster, *Celebration of Discipline* (San Francisco: Harper & Row, 1978), 79.

Chapter 2 Simplicity: To Dream the Impossible Dream

[1]Charles Wagner, *The Simple Life* (New York: McClure Phillips, 1904), 37.
[2]Ibid., 3.
[3]June McEwen, *The Gift of Simplicity* (Nashville: Broadman, 1984), 17–18.
[4]Frank Levering and Wanda Urbanska, *Simple Living* (New York: Penguin Books, 1992), 11.
[5]Ibid., 271.
[6]Niall Williams and Christine Breen, *When Summer's in the Meadow* (South Royalton, Vt.: Soho Press, 1989), 1–2, 25, 211.
[7]Levering and Urbanska, *Simple Living,* 271.

Chapter 3 Ready, Fire, Aim!

[1]Stephen R. Covey, *The Seven Habits of Highly Effective People* (New York: Simon & Schuster, 1989), 98.
[2]Ibid., 106.

[3]Thomas G. Pettepiece, *Visions of a World Hungry* (Nashville: Upper Room, 1979), as quoted in Reuben P. Job and Norman Shawchuck, *A Guide to Prayer* (Nashville: Upper Room, 1983), 116–17.

[4]Jonathan Edwards, *The Works of Jonathan Edwards*, 2 vols. (Reprint, Carlisle, Pa.: Banner of Truth Trust, 1976), 1:XX.

Chapter 4 The Simplicity of Forgiveness

[1]*The Prison Meditations of Father Alfred Delp* (New York: Herder and Herder, 1963).

[2]Ibid., 189–90.

[3]Charles Stanley, *The Gift of Forgiveness* (Nashville: Thomas Nelson, 1987), 16.

[4]C. S. Lewis, *Mere Christianity* (New York: Collier Books, 1952), 89.

[5]Louis Anderson, *Dear Dad: Letters From an Adult Child* (New York: Viking/Penguin, 1991), 15–16.

[6]Ibid., 16.

Chapter 5 Coming to Terms With Who You Are

[1]Dorothy Briggs, *Celebrate Your Self: Enhancing Your Own Self-Esteem* (Garden City, N.Y.: Doubleday, 1978).

Chapter 6 Taking Care of Yourself

[1]*Time,* January 16, 1995, 60.

[2]Quoted in George Sheehan, *Getting Fit and Feeling Great* (New York: Wings Books, 1992), 53.

[3]Ibid., 43.

[4]Ibid., 15–18.

Chapter 7 Simple Love Can Complicate Your Life

[1]Names have been changed in this chapter to protect the identity of individuals whose stories I relate.

[2]*Christianity Today,* July 19, 1993.

[3]Guest commentary, "Christian Church Should Show Caring, Compassion Toward AIDS Sufferers," *Grand Rapids Press,* December 12, 1993.

[4]W. Schuyten, "Church Mustn't Bow to Homosexual Demands," Dissent, *Grand Rapids Press,* January 7, 1994, 9A.

[5]"Network News," Grand Rapids, March 1994, 16..

Chapter 9 Enough Is Enough: The Temptation of Materialism

[1]Philip Yancey, *Money: Confronting the Power of a Modern Idol* (Portland, Ore.: Multnomah Press, 1985), 3.

[2]Randy Alcorn, *Money, Possessions and Eternity* (Wheaton, Ill.: Tyndale House, 1989).

Chapter 11 Communication: The Key to Loving God

[1]John Powell, *Fully Human, Fully Alive* (Niles, Ill.: Argus Communications, 1970), 9.

[2]John Powell, *Why Am I Afraid to Love?* (Niles, Ill.: Argus Communications, 1967).

[3]Navigators, *2:7 Series: Course 4, The Minister's Disciple* (Colorado Springs: NavPress, 1979), 19.

[4]Eugene Peterson, *Working the Angles* (Grand Rapids: Eerdmans, 1987), 32–33.

[5]Oswald Chambers, *If You Will Ask* (Grand Rapids: Discovery House. 1989), 13.

[6]Ibid., 12.

[7]*My Utmost for His Highest* and *Our Daily Bread* are available from Discovery House, a division of Radio Bible Class. *Streams in the Desert* is available from Zondervan Publishing House.

Chapter 12 Keeping Hope Alive

[1]Christiana Maslach, *Burnout: The Cost of Caring* (New York: Prentice-Hall, 1982).

What Now?

[1]Charlotte Davis Kasl, *Finding Joy: 101 Ways to Free Your Spirit and Dance with Life* (San Francisco: HarperCollins, 1994).

[2]Ibid.